When God Happens

When God Happens

Gray Temple

A
JourneyBook
from
Church Publishing Incorporated New York

Library of Congress Cataloging-in-Publication Data
    Temple, Gray, 1941-
          When God happens / Gray Temple.
                    p. cm. -- A JourneyBook
      ISBN 0898693330 (pbk.)
              1. Temple, Gray, 1941- 2. Episcopal Church--Clergy--Biography. I. Title. II. Series.

      BX5995.T38 A3 2001
      283'.092--dc21
      [B]   Episcopal
                   Church   2001047713

JourneyBook and colophon are registered trademarks of Church Publishing Incorporated.

Church Publishing Incorporated
445 Fifth Avenue
New York, NY 10016

www.churchpublishing.org

5 4 3 2 1

INTRODUCTION
. . . . . .

> Likewise the Spirit helps us in our weakness; for we do not
> know how to pray as we ought, but that very Spirit inter-
> cedes with sighs too deep for words. And God, who search-
> es the heart, knows what is the mind of the Spirit, because
> the Spirit intercedes for the saints according to the will of
> God. (Romans 8:26–27)

I'M NOT ESPECIALLY GOOD at formal prayer and I don't know much that's useful about spiritual techniques. I want to be clear about that from the beginning. There are any number of
splendid books, methods, workshops, and teachers out there who can help you with actual
procedures. What I do know is that when I go to practice lots of those procedures, past a
point my nose starts to itch and I get distracted.

By prayer we usually mean some sort of conversation between God and ourselves.
Episcopalians and others who practice regular times of addressing God (as I try to) often have
the sense of having to start the conversation off before God has really arrived in the room.
Much formal training in prayer teaches us to stay put until our hearts heat up in some fashion.
Though I work at it, I'm still not as good at that as many people I know. I wish I were.

Since prayer is conversation with God and since God is everywhere at all times in all
things, many people I know have gotten good at walking through daily life embracing all
circumstances as elements of an ongoing exchange between God and themselves. I admire
these people deeply, envy them considerably, and urge you to listen to everything they tell
you and imitate them. But, for the most part, that's not what I'll be talking about.

So, given these difficulties, why am I writing a book about prayer? Because I do know
one thing about it that's important: *God is quite good at prayer.* An essential principle in the

spiritual life is this: Make as much of your problem God's problem as you possibly can. God is delightfully competent at shouldering our difficulties with prayer.

The prayers I *can* talk about are times of actual conversation that God started with me directly—intimate conversations like you have with someone else in the room with you.

The following chapters describe a series of personal experiences, episodes in which I'm confident God took the initiative in the conversations. I recall vividly how they felt. At those times I had a sense of my personal space being penetrated and commanded as if from the outside.

Such occurrences in anyone's life are worth our knowing about. Here's why. Most of us don't quite believe God is there, or that God knows us directly. If we do believe God knows us, chances are we have trouble believing that God favors us personally. If we're active in some worshiping community, we may struggle with a sense of imposture when spiritual matters heat up. The media, from which we get an alarming proportion of our images of reality, do not display the real God in conversation with real people very often—and the few such displays they do give us are usually presented either as comic or pathological. The result is that when God in fact is self-disclosing to us, we may not recognize or trust that it's really God. We may disparage our own experiences of God. Most distressing, we may stop yearning for such engagements, dampening the hunger for God with foods that do not nourish, stones in place of bread. Overwork and overplay alike try to protect us from God's presence—or absence.

Hearing of such events in the lives of others may make us hungry and thirsty again. I find that discussing God's contacts with us amplifies the divine signal, much as my FM tuner does. Discussion alerts us to the need to pay attention to our own contact with God by asking, "Is that you?"—and then by keeping quiet. It helps us to be in discussion with others who are willing to talk about their encounters with God, provided we can trust that they're not trying to get us to sign anything. We often find ourselves saying, "Yes, something like that has happened to me as well," and even, "Mine was even better than that."

Everything in this little book is personal, drawn from stuff that has happened to me. Even so I beg that one thing be clear at the beginning: this book is not about me.

Christians are never the real heroes of their own autobiographies. This book is about God—specifically, about Jesus Christ. The encounters with Jesus I describe were usually not a response to some deliberate summons from me, as though I could whistle God up. I can't. I know some relaxing techniques of prayer—so do you—but where these encounters overlap those practices, they occurred more as interruptions than direct consequences. And my various confessors and spiritual directors would violate no confidentiality in assuring you that these occurrences were hardly divine responses to any virtue I manifest.

Communication specialists tell us that fifty-five percent of communication is the impact the communicator makes by her appearance and carriage; around thirty-five percent is the timbre and tone of the voice; only seven percent of the impact is the actual content of the message. (I'm not sure what happened to the three percent remainder.)

I will be reporting only the seven percent part of various encounters with God—the words I sensed God/Christ was conveying. Even those words are only approximate because my mind furnished them to reconstruct a wordless communication.

Though that's what I'll relay, the words were usually the least important element. I wish I had the ability to convey the other thirty-five percent, the fifty-five percent—the sense of Presence. When someone asks, "How do you know it was God?" it is to that sense of Presence that I appeal.

Quite simply I don't know how to describe the kind courtesy with which the Presence exercises unquestionable authority or the depth of charity, understanding, and acceptance evident in any divine mention of any person, even my personal enemies. God *dignifies* everything and everyone God mentions. I don't know how to convey the playful, affectionate tone of the sternest rebuke—and our own sense of being honored even as we're getting severely corrected. How are we to know that God's harshest judgments are friendlier than our own most lavish self-praise?

My hope is that somehow the words themselves might reconstitute their speaker's Presence as you read.

In offering you a series of episodes so personal and suggesting that you use them to reflect on your own, I know I risk seeming to offer my experiences as some sort of yardstick. I don't think my life is much of a measure for anyone else's. In this respect I'm reminded of Mark Twain's observation that anyone can serve others as a bad example.

God's contact with us is so vital to us, it's so important that it be true, that we feel the strong need to protect ourselves against any inauthenticity, any effort on his part to capture us for his own agenda. I'll try to filter out as much of my own personal imperialism as possible, but you'll have to do most of it since so much of it is unconscious.

Paul told us that the Holy Spirit comes to our aid when we've reached the limit of our ability—or willingness—to pray. When we think we've hit the wall in prayer, it's not over. Though I don't have anything novel to contribute by way of technique, I have gleaned some insights over the decades into how we can expect the Spirit to help us. Let me offer them here, since the bulk of our conversation will be more anecdotal than theoretical.

First, in an important sense, the Spirit has already come to our aid—in our very creation. God created you and me for prayer.

Who designed and made your skull? God did. Does God want you to know God's presence? The combined witnesses of the Bible, the record of the saints, and those around us encourage us to think the answer to that question is yes.

Will that answer require your brain to be aware of God's presence? Eventually, yes.

So consider this: if God wants your brain to be aware of the Presence, do you think your God-crafted skull is so thick that God can't get through to it? Don't you think God designed access ports into your personal space?

Let's get more specific. In 1997, researchers at the University of California in San Diego studied brain patterns of epileptics who were experiencing mystical peak experiences while they were having seizures.* They found that the right temporal lobe "lights up" during such experiences. Just for fun they also wired up a group of Pentecostals and others who report dramatic encounters with God. As the latter described their experiences, the same right temporal lobe lit up. The researchers started talking about "the God Spot" during their coffee breaks.

It looks like a specific zone of our brains functions as an "antenna to God." That means each of us is already wired up for prayer—hardwired in our neurons.

Second, the simplest preparation for knowing the presence of God as you pray is to want to. Simple as it is, that's more difficult than it looks. That is, it helps that it's *God* I want, not just some specific fruit of divine favor.

For example: I'm typing this paragraph in the Atlanta airport before dawn, one of fifty-five standby passengers on a heavily over-sold flight. I'm praying that God will slip me past the others—the others who are glowering at my clerical garb with the superstitious suspicion that I possess unfair supernatural pull. (I'm due at two meetings later today in a distant city, wrestling with problems that have no ready solutions, with people I don't know too well, expecting to come away having to raise large sums of money.) As I sit here wanting that seat, praying for it, resenting my rivals, the presence of God is difficult to feel. But as I step back from my specific desire and ask simply to be aware of God's presence in this airport, the whole atmosphere on this concourse changes. The people seem more attractive, surprisingly "dear," though that's a word that doesn't often occur to me. I wouldn't trade this moment for a business-class seat to Paris.

Third, There's no getting around the utility of routine and regularity in prayer. A wise friend once told me, "God does not usually appear *during* your quiet time; God usually

* Ray Kurzweil. *The Age of Spiritual Machines: When Computers Exceed Human Intelligence* (New York: Viking Press 1999) 150.

. . . . . .

appears *because of* your quiet time." And there's an advantage to your regular time of prayer occurring first thing in the morning. What you do with your mind for the first half hour after waking sets the emotional tenor of the entire day. If you begin your day wishing for your heart to rub against the heart of God, you will live out the day with enhanced sensitivity to God's presence.

Fourth, how can you tell if it's really God and not just your own thoughts or wishes? God's presence always manifests certain unmistakable—and unfakeable—characteristics. Any mention God makes about you or about another person (even your enemy) will be suffused with an utterly understanding charity, an affectionate comprehension that dignifies everyone—even you. Voltaire remarked, "*Tout comprendre, c'est tout pardoner*"—"To understand everything is to forgive everything." Only in God's real presence does that make its full sense.

When I'm just thinking something through—maybe "stewing" would be a more accurate description—it's as though my thoughts are two-dimensional, black-and-white. But sometimes, when they suddenly go three-dimensional and Technicolor, I know God has taken over.

At such a time, I may get insight into somebody's circumstances. The way I can tell if God is the source is that God never gives me critical or negative information about another person. Not ever. Anything God discloses about another person is always an expression of love, never anything that would empower me to another's disadvantage.

Another marker for God's authentic presence is an authority, however warm, that brooks no *lèse majesté*. The only tolerable posture in that actual presence is respectful, trusting *brokenness*. There is no confusion about who is who. I think that the encounter clears up any doubt about prayer being simply a way of talking to ourselves or about "spirituality" being limited to a cultivated self-refinement. If that's a zone of myself emerging at such times, it's certainly not the self I'm usually aware of carrying around.

As you'll notice in the following anecdotes, I began by asking for some quite specific favors from God. I actually got a lot of them, though even when I haven't, the prayer has been worthwhile. I think requesting favors is a good way to pray. "Lord, Won't You Buy Me A Mercedes Benz" is a perfectly agreeable way to *begin* a prayer—as long as we understand that prayer is a conversation rather than an exchange of telegrams. That is, when I pray for a Lexus—and stay on the line—I wind up grateful for my Honda, discussing my driving habits with the Most High.

I confess to you without embarrassment that I routinely pray for myself. Virtually everything our Lord teaches us about prayer assumes that we are praying for ourselves. This understanding is the necessary entry into the confidence to pray for others. Refusing to do so based on some notion that it's not spiritual enough is trying to be more spiritual than Jesus himself—and that's a racket.

Yet over the years I've noticed a shift in the direction my prayers take. The posture of respectful trusting brokenness I mentioned earlier eventually leads to an appreciative exploration of what is alongside pleading for what I wish might be.

The exploration takes a couple of forms. If nothing particular feels urgent, I feel drawn to survey the present time with gratitude, in Jesus' name blessing all that is. But when a situation does feel urgent or anguished, increasingly I feel drawn simply to ask Jesus to join me in it, to share his own reaction to things with me, to allow his presence to interpret what's going on, to inform its meaning. Just as I've learned not to ask Jesus to fix my brokenness—it's my antenna posture, after all—I often feel little impulse to ask Jesus to fix my surroundings.

I missed the flight. They're holding the meetings without me. At the moment I'm in my favorite restaurant in Atlanta writing to you while awaiting a dear friend who happened to be loose for lunch— and nobody knows I'm in town until tomorrow night.

What's to fix?

. . . . . .

IN THE FALL OF 1957, I was in the fourth form—what normal people call the tenth grade—at Groton School. It was my third year as a student on a generous scholarship at America's premier prep school.

My great uncle, a prominent statesman from North Carolina, had drawn my dad aside and advised that if my brothers and I were to be Southerners, we each needed to spend some portion of our education outside the region—especially in that post-'54 day and time. That conversation resulted in my going w-a-a-a-a-y outside the region in more senses than merely geographic.

Groton was (and remains) a strange and wonderful place. Though comprising sons of extraordinarily wealthy families from all over the world, its Spartan regimen reduced us all to a common economic level. We slept in barely furnished cubicles, not rooms. We shaved and brushed our teeth each morning from decades-old tin washbasins, perhaps the very basins used by FDR or Dean Acheson. The dress was coat-and-tie all day with white shirts required from dinner to bedtime. We went to chapel eight times a week for a full Book of Common Prayer service. (I once calculated that if each chapel service counted for a Sunday observance, I would not have to go back to church until I was ninety-two.)

To excel, you didn't have to be wealthy—merely athletically courageous and intellectually adventurous. They taught Southerners to ice-skate by strapping skates on us, thrusting us onto the rink, poking at us with hockey sticks until we lost our tempers, forgot we couldn't skate, and charged after them. It worked.

And the school took its New England Episcopalianism seriously. By the second form we were studying the Bible by the historical-critical method (respectfully), learning all about "Q" (a hypothetical collection of Jesus' sayings underlying Matthew and Luke), the primacy of Mark among the first three gospels, and about how Moses likely didn't write the

. . . . . .

Torah, which is actually a weft of independent documents referred to by biblical scholars as J, E, P, and D. Pretty grown-up stuff for high school.

My first personal encounter with Jesus Christ grew out of a sacred studies class. The previous week, without my noticing, my brain had been posed a puzzle. I'd been trying to squeeze out the crowded door of sacred studies, free at last from a lecture on the four Ecumenical Councils leading to the Chalcedonian Formula on the two natures of Christ. (In the tenth grade! No joke!) A classmate was prating on and on, something to the effect, "Of course, *I* could discourse for hours on the relation of the Son to the Father . . . ." (At times Groton felt like being caught on a nuclear sub with a debate team.) I was annoyed—yet at least part of my annoyance was the realization that *I* couldn't.

Until. . . .

It was sometime after midnight. It occurred in my five-by-ten sleeping cubicle.

Something woke me up in the darkness of the silent dormitory. I became aware of a bright source of light just outside my field of vision, a light so bright I sensed it would be a mistake to try to look upward. It dawned on me that this event, while quite real, might not be photographable, but I was not frightened—yet. I was more curious than scared, I recall. Then a basketball-sized globe of light seemed to detach itself from the larger light source. It floated down to the foot of my bed and hovered there. In the middle of my curiosity I was struck with the notion, "Well, this answers whether I can discourse on the relation of the Son to the Father; I guess I can . . . ." Somehow I knew I was looking at a metaphorical visualization of that relation.

But then things heated up and it quit being conceptual. The globe of light began to move. It floated to my right and then along the side of my bed towards my head. As it approached, it became more and more . . . personal. A lifetime of attending church services and Sunday school finally served me: I knew this was Jesus.

What was personal about the light? I was aware—I don't know how—that my thoughts were absolutely totally accessible to him. Furthermore, at least some of his thoughts were accessible to me. They were simply there in my head in the form of deep understandings, deeper than anything I'd known before.

I was aware of being absolutely accepted and delighted in. That may sound clichéd. But remember, I was in my third year at the country's most competitive prep school, a Southern scholarship boy among Yankee classmates who could buy my whole town with their walking-around money. Acceptance was at something of a premium. And here it was.

I sensed that if this person were the center forward on my soccer team, I'd be the bravest right halfback in New England. I sensed that this person wanted me to know that we had always known each other and been connected. I agreed with that, though I could not think of how it might be true.

Oddly, for a moment a lot of theological abstract terms bandied about in sacred studies class—all the "–tion" words, like redemption and sanctification, made luminous, personal, existential sense.

In later years, looking back on that event, I've wished I'd been raised something like a Southern Baptist. At least then I'd have known what to say. Something like, "Come into my heart." Or, "Be my Savior and Lord." Maybe this encounter could have made some abiding difference then. As it was, I grew frightened of being overwhelmed, of being absorbed. When you are new to joy—or to love from someone who doesn't have to love you—it can terrify you. It did me. (How often since then I've wished I could go back and get overwhelmed or absorbed!) I whispered something like, "I'm mighty glad you're there—now I believe I'll just go to sleep for a little while." I tucked my head under the pillow in order to evade the Presence of Jesus and, for the first time in my life, went to sleep on purpose.

I awakened maybe fifteen minutes later and peeped out. He was gone.

He stayed gone a long time.

· · · · · ·

THE ENCOUNTER WITH JESUS at Groton left me persuaded of the truth of the Christian proclamation, but it made no discernable difference to my character or my inner life. Nothing about it, for example, slowed my headlong splash into the University of North Carolina's Olympian social activities. I took few courses I didn't already know a lot about, so I wasted little time in study or in cultivating righteous study habits.

Life at Chapel Hill felt wonderfully merry until my junior year. That fall two circumstances converged, seriously derailing my idyllic existence.

I encountered course work that required fresh effort. Suddenly anytime I cut a class, it resulted in noticeable lacunae in my grasp of the topic. Moreover I'd developed casual habits of class attendance. Now there were nasty consequences.

At about the same time, I was lured away from a humdrum dating relationship by a vibrant "Lady In Red" type against whose charms I found myself helpless and clueless. By the end of the semester I was seriously in over my head, drawn much further into sexual exploration than my Puritan conscience could sort out.

A couple of weeks prior to semester finals, I awoke to find myself in bad trouble: academic, relational, and psychological.

Nowadays when I hear people refer to "nervous breakdowns" I think I know what they mean. For two days I was immobilized, spending hours trembling on my bed, afraid to go out, afraid to be with other people. I felt as though my brain were poisoned, squeezing toxins into the rest of my shaking body. (I say "brain" instead of "mind" quite deliberately. The misery was so stark it felt organic, physical.)

The University Health Service operated an inpatient psychiatric facility, the dreaded South Wing. I didn't know what went on there, but I was certain that nobody who went in ever came back out. At best I would be looking down the barrel of a lifetime of filling out

· · · · · ·

forms that asked, "Have you ever been treated for mental illness? Supply details on a separate sheet. . . ."

I knew I had to get well or my life was over. As I lay shaking on my bed I thought seriously about crawling onto the roof ledge outside my fraternity house bedroom window, taking one of the shards of broken glass with which it was littered, and cutting myself beyond recovery. Nero had done it; so had Petronius; it might not be that bad. . . .

As I was considering suicide, I cried out to God, saying something like, "My brain has something broken in it. You made my brain. You know how it's supposed to work. If you don't fix it, my life is over."

Within seconds serenity flowed over me and filled me, starting in my abdomen and moving in both directions, salving my diseased brain. It reminded me of the time that night at prep school—it was like the effect of that Presence, only this time without the visual sensations.

There was only one personal exchange as the soothing took place: without hearing an actual voice, my head was filled with a personal message: *"Do not forget what any of this felt like."*

At the time I didn't understand that instruction. Not a week goes by these days without my understanding it clearly.

THE DIVINE INTERVENTION that pulled me out of that mental health crisis in my junior year catapulted me into hanging onto my grade-point average. Serenity during an exam is a great asset—especially if your information is thin.

The "Lady In Red" mercifully decided to pick on someone her own size and started dating wealthier, more experienced guys on remote campuses—an answer to a prayer I hadn't had the sense to pray. With much of the internal pressure relieved, I reflected on the fact that it was time to stop drifting through life—which for me at the time meant college life with no goal in view. I began wondering if I could put the university on hold for a while. The problem was that my scholarship program didn't have student sabbaticals built into its provisions. If I dropped out, I could probably come back—but it would no longer be paid for.

About that time the university advertised interviews for two yearlong exchange scholarships to Göttingen University in West Germany.

I felt an inward stirring to apply. The idea of a year in Germany felt deep, dark, and romantic. To one born just prior to America's entry into World War II the very name Germany caused a slight *frisson* of danger. Somehow it seemed that a year in Germany would give me the chance to face all sorts of darknesses, my own at the top of the list. So I put my name in.

When I showed up for the interview I was wired and jittery, out to sell myself to the committee, making it inescapably obvious that I was their man. The interview went poorly. My approach, not surprisingly, proved over the top for a couple of key committee members. The committee selected a friend of mine for the first slot but the second remained unawarded. I was told that I would have to return for a second interview the following week. Recalling the last time I had felt this wretched and needy, I decided to try prayer again. I offered the second deliberate prayer of my undergraduate career. I asked

. . . . .

God—no, I *begged* God—to allow me to go to Germany on that scholarship.

The night before the second interview, an appeal went out to fraternities on our campus for donations of blood in response to a gruesome multi-car accident over on the campus of Duke University. A friend grabbed me and said, "Come on, Temple. Let's go donate blood."

Now I don't like needles a lot, especially ones they leave in you while they go out for coffee. And in those days you didn't just fill up a little plastic sack—you got hooked up to a glass bottle that looked like it would hold a quart. My first thought, not atypically, was about myself. I needed all my strength for the next evening's grilling by the Göttingen scholarship committee. But not wanting to appear chicken-hearted to my friend, I replied, "Okay, sure."

Off we drove. We found the blood lab at Duke Hospital. Onto the table . . . brisk alcohol rub on arm . . . needle into vein . . . sweat dripping off forehead . . . sharp ache in forearm . . . hope my friend can't see how pale I am . . . hope the nurse doesn't get alarmed at my pallor and start shouting . . . why on earth am I doing this. . . ?

The next day was dreamlike. I think I understood where the old medical practice of bleeding might have come from. George Washington's doctor probably recommended the same treatment for pre-battle jitters. I wafted into the interview room, calm and mellow, laconic, deeply tranquil. No question could rile me—I simply lacked the energy.

■ ■ ■

They called later that night. The scholarship was mine. My former critics had been impressed with my poise.

And as I whooped and hollered down the hall from the phone, I felt myself in the presence of One who was laughing.

· · · · · ·

FOR ME THE YEAR AT GÖTTINGEN was a delightful time of growing up. With an ocean lying between me and the guarantors of my conscience, I come to realize that there were better reasons for self-discipline and right behavior than the fact that my parents or schoolmasters required them.

But for the United States 1963 and 1964 was a time of anguish and struggle—President Kennedy's assassination, followed by President Johnson's push for the Civil Rights bill. I watched the President's funeral and police attacks on Civil Rights marchers on a snowy black-and-white TV, acutely aware of every inch of ocean between me and home. I was miserably homesick and my classmates didn't help. The burden of proof lay with me to prove that I was not an overt racist. The other students watched me narrowly as I interacted with my new friend Daniel, a classmate from Nigeria. Still struggling with their own recent history, German students of that day were not about to let an American Southerner off easy.

I'd been away from active involvement in the Civil Rights struggle for a whole year when I returned home for my senior year. Though I had previously been somewhat active— once placing my college scholarship on the line in defense of a fellow scholarship holder who had been arrested during a march in Selma and was in danger of losing his stipend (he'd broken the law of the land, you see)—I was now uncertain how to connect. Student leadership and the public issues themselves had changed quickly and thoroughly during my absence.

One day God settled it.

It was a Saturday morning and the autumn air was electric with tension. A racially integrated parade was scheduled to proceed down Franklin Street, the main street in Chapel Hill, to protest the many businesses that remained segregated. Along with several of my fraternity brothers, I drifted downtown to watch. I went as much out of curiosity as anything.

. . . . . .

Before the parade started, a large crowd of spectators lined the sidewalk—waiting. The mood was bellicose and raucous, catcalls and shouted slogans filled the air, lots of beer was sloshing around even at that hour of the morning.

As the march slowly made its way up the street to the beat of a somber drum that seemed to gather all our pulses, the crowd around me grew louder, more restive, and surlier. They started flinging beer cans, trash, and curses out into the parade. Among the marchers was one man I knew—the YMCA chaplain; he smiled at me nervously, as if he expected me to throw something at him.

That's when God happened. A friend standing beside me—the same friend who had dragged me to give blood two years earlier—muttered, "I believe I'll take a walk," and stepped into the parade, leaving me isolated in that hooting crowd.

All of a sudden a question formed itself inside me, a wordless question that nonetheless filled my mind: *"If the Russians were to drop the bomb right this minute, which crowd would you rather die in?"*

I knew the answer. I knew who asked.

I stepped off the curb into the parade.

PEOPLE ARE OFTEN CURIOUS about how a preacher knows the "call" to enter seminary and eventually the ordained ministry. Few of us can give an accurate account of our "calls," but let me try to tell you why I went to seminary right after college.

Like many repressed intellectual kids, the closest I could get to ecstatic emotion was the breakthrough "Aha! experience" I often felt during study when I sensed an intellectual connection forming. And for me these occurred most often when studying humanistic psychology, the philosophy of religion, and great literary works (like Dostoyevsky) when they'd verge onto spiritual topics. How exciting it would be to pursue a career where you got to do that all the time. I decided I wanted to be a theologian. The path to that career led through seminary, ordination, and on to graduate study. So I entered Virginia Theological Seminary in Alexandria in 1965, intent on adding degrees after graduation.

Seminary fed my mind, but my soul went hungry—and in those days I didn't know my soul well enough to tell the difference. I wish I had declared to the faculty that I was there to discover a personal and disciplined relationship with God—but I didn't know that myself. There were some members of the faculty who could have helped. I wish I'd said as much to my classmates—any number of them could have coached me. But I had no words to ask for what I needed.

Chapel services did little to heat my spirit. Those were the final days of the 1928 Prayer Book, just before the church at large began the experiments that led to the 1979 Book of Common Prayer. Chapel embodied all the spirituality of a drill team, its dominant characteristic self-conscious seriousness.

For most of my time in seminary I assumed I was headed for an academic career, putting up with fieldwork in a local parish only for the meager income.

. . . . . .

That all changed abruptly during the day of the assassination of Dr. Martin Luther King Jr.

The seminary community, of course, grieved over King's death and was horrified by the televised images of the riots, burnings, and looting taking place in Washington, D.C. right across the Potomac from us. But northern Virginia remained calm, unaffected by our nation's capital turning into an occupied city overnight.

Jack, a layman in my fieldwork parish, awakened me early the next morning with a phone call. "Thanks to your sermon on Christian involvement in social justice a few months ago, I've been volunteering in a Methodist church in a black neighborhood downtown. The block has been wiped-out. The church is serving as an emergency shelter and food distribution center. They need volunteers. Your sermon got me into this and you're coming with me." Within an hour we entered an unfamiliar and frightening country. Washington D.C. resembled nothing so much as an occupied banana republic, every intersection guarded by heavily armored police, airborne divisions, National Guard units, Civil Air Patrol in uniforms—even Explorer Scouts. We threaded past checkpoint after checkpoint, Jack managing to talk us through each one. The soldiers mostly showed flared nostrils and lots of eye white, except for the airborne troops whose steely alertness did nothing to reduce the intolerable tension felt everywhere.

The unscathed brick exterior of the church presented a surreal contrast to the acrid smoke, detritus, abandoned and smoldering automobiles around it. It was a still point, and the surrounding pandemonium slowly began to organize itself into rough order. People—black and white—scurried around shouting instructions at each other, yelling for help with tasks they'd grabbed for themselves, food was being hauled off army trucks—somehow getting sorted, stacked, and stored for distribution. Volunteers commandeered telephones to field calls from panicked households needing food and medical attention. Jack and I served as runners for hours at a time, schlepping boxes of food and medicine to the surviving housing units, dodging the military patrols after curfew.

· · · · · ·

The band of volunteers—an unlikely team if ever there was one—developed a spirit that made tireless and sometimes frightening efforts increasingly joyous as, with little conscious design, a system began to emerge among us. We were a motley crew: my friend Jack, a Department of Agriculture bureaucrat; myself, an intellectual seminarian; dozens of men and women of both races and all ages. A soldier went AWOL and joined us; to redirect army food trucks to our shelter he altered his uniform to look like an officer.

As I've said, I'd always been casual about class attendance, but that week took the prize. I'd told no one on campus I was leaving; classmates and teachers were so used to my absences that Jean (my wife by then) said it took several days before worried phone calls began. Still there was one seminar in theology I couldn't miss since it met only once a week. I simply had to return to northern Virginia for a couple of hours. Jack lent me his car. It was daytime so I didn't have much trouble getting through barriers and checkpoints.

Oddly, the seminary seemed to lack any real notion of what was taking place just a few miles from its serene campus. Nobody was talking about it. Coming back felt stranger than leaving. I found I was virtually aphasic, stricken speechless in that once comfortable setting. I lurked in the seminar, uncharacteristically silent. Before the bell stopped ringing, I was back in Jack's car, and driving as fast as conditions permitted to the place that had become my church.

Reentering Washington, I realized several things. First, I was startled at how rapidly I had come to love my colleagues at the shelter—and how deeply. In an emergency it does not take long to bond sturdily. Years later I came to understand that this is the work of the Holy Spirit. Second, I realized that this was not white people helping black people: this was the people of God serving the children of God. Third, it hit me that this most life-giving encounter with spirit and Spirit was the fruit of parish work—not academic study. At that moment, the allure of being a theologian began to lose its grip on me. Fourth, I realized that, except for the time back on campus, I had felt the personal Presence subtly for the last few days. That Presence abided for several days more until the acute crisis passed.

The next Sunday—Palm Sunday—it felt over. We waved goodbye to the congregation gathered for worship, and dispersed with hugs, warm smiles, and tears.

I look back on my seminary years today with gratitude and affection. I continue to love and admire my classmates and their families. I reckon those years among the richest intellectual and fraternal periods of my life.

But God happened for me most forcibly the week I left seminary and crossed the river.

. . . . . .

A WELTER OF MOTIVES led me to ordained ministry, many of them unconscious. Yet a personal brush with God that night at Groton had been at the core of my decision.

The Standing Committee of my sponsoring diocese tried to get me to reflect on my motives, but I staved them off. The seminary admissions director tried too, as did my bishop, and the church-mandated psychiatrist. All these people tried to expose me to some of the other forces battling within me over and apart from brushes with God, knowing that if I went too far in the ministry without getting my motives clear, those hidden forces would inevitably catch up with me. There was a lot I didn't want to look at: notably a large need for being loved that could only get stroked by being recognized as a leader. I felt as if all those interviewers were my natural enemies. My job was to make them all want me ordained, to agree to my suitability. I quickly learned to be cagey about my original sense of being with God in these interviews, since the first couple of times I mentioned it my listeners weren't as impressed as I thought they should have been. Face one roomful of knowing smiles after you've just said, "God called me," and you learn not to mention *that* again. I learned to discuss "my spirituality" at some length—but that was hardly the same thing. I jumped through the hoops and tried to slip through the filters. I figured that when I was finally in seminary I'd get to be as "religious" as I once felt at my best moments.

In seminary I quickly learned that raw enthusiasm for God (not that I was all that overtly enthusiastic) is not admired per se—it has to be tempered with a rigorous grasp of the theoretical, historical, cognitive, and practical realities of life within the flawed People of God in the midst of a flawed world. For example, having to learn that the Bible is not purely history in our modern sense jolted some of my classmates—but I noticed anyone looked jolted by this news lost points, so I made sure I didn't. Again I got cagey, thinking that once I got out into my own temporary ministry, biding a couple of years before graduate school, wearing collars and dark suits, embodying, in effect, permission to be spiritual, I could get as religious as I'd like to be. However, at that moment it was essential to be cool.

Ultimately, I graduated, got ordained, and hit my congregation, a small mission church on the campus of Appalachian State University in Boone, North Carolina. Campus work was fun and easy—I'd been born and bred in that brier patch. But my collision with the lay congregation was, by far, the most abrasive church experience I had encountered thus far.

Congregations usually welcome fresh clergy warmly when they first arrive, but for reasons as complex and unconscious as those that impelled new priests to ordination. Nobody makes them face into their mixed motives. I quickly discovered that few people were interested in my spirituality—far less in my (as yet unexpressed) religious yearnings.

I still shudder when I recall walking into the sacristy of my tiny church, interrupting the imperious head of the Altar Guild raging at a tremulous, weepy volunteer for ironing and folding a communion napkin incorrectly. My suggestion to the women (who were probably twice my age) that altar service has to do with the service of God and that hollering at each other didn't fit only made both women my implacable enemies.

My attempts to enlist the vestry in prayer before we addressed the practicalities of leaky roofs and scanty budgets were met with the incredulous scorn my inexperience deserved. Any hopes I'd harbored that God had much to do with parish administration were best kept to myself. Apparently a congregation was no better place for a young priest to try to be religious in than seminary had been.

The need to appear wise and composed forced me to cultivate a self-consciousness that militated against sensing God's presence. A lot of recently ordained clergy are two-legged fictions—God knows *I* was—and I don't think God reads fiction. It is said that a priest needs three things for success: glasses for the look of intelligence, graying hair for the look of wisdom, and a hemorrhoid for the look of constant concern. I lacked all three.

. . . . . .

So without my noticing, I woke up one morning realizing that I'd missed the point of the ordained ministry. My doings during the day had more to do with survival than with promoting God's Kingdom. I wouldn't have recognized the Kingdom if it had bitten me. My youthful glimpses of personal closeness to God had dumped me into a dead end, a trap. Not only was personal contact with God not available—and had not been since those few moments in college—I feared that if God were to restore contact, the result might be equally devastating.

Being fairly bright and an energetic achiever, I wasn't content to suffer my crisis sitting still. I needed to take action. I crafted myself new understandings of what I was doing as a priest—I addressed myself to the emotional needs of the students I served as chaplain, and to the turmoil that wracked our society at the peak of the Vietnam War. Specialties in counseling and in political organizing seemed to protect me in the face of the terrifying *generality* of the priesthood.

I thus became a political and social activist—and got real, real busy at it. Prayer formed no part of that ministry—the gospel mandate for justice was clear enough direction for me. Prayer would just slow it down and was suspect for that very reason. I saw prayer as evasive.

If God is really good at prayer, if God is really skilled at penetrating the personal space of a human creature, how can God emerge into the life of one who has become scared of spirituality itself, into the life of one who is even heartbroken by it?

The Thermostat

. . . . . .

I THINK GOD GETS CLERGY to loosen our collars by turning up the heat. Certainly God does little to keep things cool. For the first few years in Boone, the mounting heat on me came from the outside in the form of external opposition. But I can take any amount of that kind of heat—it just baked me harder.

I'm good at turning opposition into an oblique compliment. "A man is known by his enemies." Yep. It's easy to feel superior to a loosely wrapped Altar Guild director who goes into rages over folds in the linens and to then pose as a virtuous martyr before her artless public attacks. Congregants and townspeople who disagreed with my pacifist posture among university students could be dismissed as sub-Christian reactionaries. People who didn't want to hear my opinion on local race relations every Sunday were clearly racists. People who opposed my efforts to ensure reproductive rights for women students were obviously repressed Puritans. Good enemies, all in all. A priest could take a lot of satisfaction from such enemies. "So treated they the Prophets which were before you," as somebody said.

Periodically "Charismatic" or "born-again" types would visit my congregation. They neither stayed long nor left quietly. I was proud of that—my gospel clearly wasn't for everybody.

So God turned up the *internal* heat.

A farmer once said, "They say, 'You can lead a horse to water but you can't make him drink.' But *I* know how to make him drink—feed him *salt*."

God salted me in a couple of ways. I was reading a lot of Gandhi and Martin Luther King, Jr., identifying my mission of opposing the war in Vietnam and the draft with their famous protest campaigns. As I read, an almost undetectable Presence in the room began whispering to me that each of those men had been primarily a contemplative, only secondarily an activist. Through his lengthy periods of fasting and prayer Gandhi learned to love the British—sort of—and Dr. King regarded Bull Connor with compassion. By contrast I was in flight from anything prayerful or contemplative. Whereas Gandhi and King were actuated by love for their enemies, I was actuated by contempt for Richard Nixon, Henry Kissinger, and Generals Westmoreland and Lewis B. Hershey.

Yet I began to understand that without cultivating an interior life I could not pretend to take part in the company of my heroes. One day in an effort to get spiritual I walked across my study, took a book on prayer off the shelf intent on mastering this prayer business—tried it, hit the wall, and bounced. The silence terrified me, as did stillness. And I found simply reciting the daily Morning or Evening Prayer services from the Book of Common Prayer unendurably boring. So I reached the logical conclusion—I had tried prayer, and had to live with the knowledge that I couldn't do it.

God further salted my tongue with tacky, Charismatic, born-again people who occasionally visited the church. To be sure, they were usually embarrassingly anti-intellectual; their political opinions were crepuscular; their taste in music and their yearning for liturgical dance made my flesh crawl. And yet . . . whenever they talked about Jesus, they spoke of him personally, not abstractly. Surprisingly their words reactivated my introduction to him from years past. I recognized him in their talk. I realized I could not recognize him in my own talk or in that of colleagues. This wasn't how it was supposed to be.

All this combined to form an inexorable pressure. I ready to explode.

I felt the first rumbles at a diocesan clergy conference I'd helped organize. At one point I was in a discussion group with a priest named Jim Radebaugh and his wife Joy, both notorious for being "Charismatics." Somebody said something I adjudged overly pious and clichéd, likely some reference to "the Precious Blood." By way of reply I suggested that such treacly talk wasn't fit for grown-ups. Joy looked me square in the eye and remarked softly, "Gray, when you develop some spiritual maturity, you may realize they were right in what they said." Jim just smiled gently without comment. Their quiet acceptance ignited my temper. "Don't patronize me, lady!" I bellowed.

"I'm not patronizing you, Gray—I'm telling you the truth," she replied. She raised her voice not at all.

In an anguish of indissoluble rage, I fled the conference a day early and tore off to the home of a friend, begging for privacy on his back deck. My friend astutely gauged my condition, nodded without comment, fetched me a stiff bourbon, and left me to my struggle.

I sat there slugging down whisky, going over my exchange with the Radebaughs again and again, trying to make it come out better, looking for some obvious error in Joy's observation—without success. Suddenly, the internal pressure burst through the surface. I found I was weeping, weeping hard.

And the Presence was there on that deck, somewhere behind me. I knew better than to turn around.

"It won't always hurt this bad, Gray."

The Roller Coaster

· · · · · ·

I DROVE THE LONG MILES HOME from my friend's deck in a dark funk, ruminating on the possibility of leaving the ordained ministry, beginning to sense I was not suited to it. The events of the clergy conference had left me feeling that I was somehow an imposter.

How would I tell Jean? She'd had enough struggle with my entering the ministry back when we were courting—being a preacher's daughter, she'd had little appetite to get back into that life. Over the last five years she had writhed in frustration at my nightly reports of various conflicts in the congregation and on campus, helpless herself to engage my opponents directly. How would she feel about my abandoning it? I wasn't sure.

As I entered the kitchen door, Jean told me I'd had an emergency phone call from a woman named Polly, a recovering alcoholic, as plain-spoken as they come. After greeting Jean only briefly, I returned Polly's call.

"Gray, my sister just called from a hospital in Greensboro. She's dying. She has less than a week. She's the only person on earth I love as much as I do my daughter. I can't stand this. Get over here."

"I can't, Polly," I replied. "I'm quitting the ministry."

A silence.

"Have you officially quit yet?"

"Not yet. I'm telling the bishop tomorrow."

"So is my tithe money still in your pocket?"

"Well, if you put it like that. . . ."

"Then get your sorry tail over here right now!"

I did as she told me.

Ignoring my petulant misery, Polly told me she wanted me to pray for her sister, evidently hoping for some sort of miracle. I told her frankly that I had no clue as to how to pray or

· · · · · ·

if prayer worked. At any rate, I assured her, I hadn't been able to pray for a long time. I felt as sorry as I could be that her sister was dying, but I wasn't going to fake a prayer.

"I pay you to pray, you wimp! Now do your damn job."

"Tell you what I'll do," I replied. "Let's sit here together and not talk for a while. I'll see if I can fetch some sort of prayer—and you pray for me to be able to." She nodded.

We sat in silence for about fifteen minutes—I wasn't watching any clocks. At length I felt braced to talk aloud to the room's empty air. It came out something like this: "God, I used to think I knew you and I really believed you were there. All that's gone now, and I feel stupid even trying. But if you are there, and if there is something you can do about Polly's sister, we need you to do it—because we're out of resources."

I believe that was the first time in my life that I had ever prayed with another human being without a prayer book between us, though that didn't strike me at the time.

I looked up to see tears flowing down Polly's face. Fecklessly I tried to say something consoling, about how hard it must be to sit helpless while someone she loves was slipping away from her forever.

"You ass," replied Polly, "I'm not crying from grief—I just had a vision!"

"A VISION!" I gasped. "What of?"

"I saw my sister sitting up in her hospital bed! She was surrounded with a pure light. She had a smile on her face I haven't seen since we were kids! I don't know what the outcome of this cancer is going to be. I'm not really sure I care right this minute. But my sister is all right. And she's going to *stay* all right!"

· · · · ·

POLLY HUGGED ME HARD at the door as I left. She would drive to Greensboro the next morning to remain with her sister until the end. I realized I wanted to see this through—something here was for *me* as well as Polly and her sister, something important that connected to my despair. I told Polly I would drive over to Greensboro the next afternoon as soon as I could clear my calendar. (She tactfully neglected to ask if I was still going to call the bishop.)

At my office the next morning, I realized I had two problems. First, Jean had left that morning for a two-day trip out of town, taking our only car. Second, I was chicken. I knew I was into something real weird, over which I had little control.

I made two phone calls. The first was to a parishioner to borrow an automobile for a couple of days. The second was to a priest in another city. Bill had been working on me gently for several years to explore the power of the Holy Spirit in my life and ministry. I hadn't blown him off—but only because his political views lined up with mine. I described what was going on with Polly and her sister, coinciding with my personal despair about priesthood and the spiritual chaos my tangle with Joy Radebaugh had compelled me to own. Bill prayed with me over the phone—the first time in my life anyone had—and advised me simply to be open to things as they unfolded.

Halfway down the highway from Boone to Greensboro, I realized I had a third problem—a bad one. I had no idea what hospital Polly's sister was in; I didn't know the sister's last name; and I had no idea where Polly was staying. Hopeless.

Oddly, it felt like I'd driven too far to turn back.

At that moment I remembered an anecdote I'd heard Bishop Gordon of Alaska recount years earlier. He'd spoken of an Eskimo who flew to Seattle for a meeting without knowing its exact location. Upon arrival he had prayed for God to get him to the meeting, and,

· · · · ·

trusting some sort of internal guidance, had walked up to the right door. The story had annoyed me at the time—evidently enough to stick in my memory.

So I said aloud, "God, you know this city and its hospitals and you know Polly's sister. Please connect us."

On the outskirts of Greensboro was one of those signs with a big H on it, signaling directions to a hospital. I followed it.

I pulled into the hospital parking lot and stepped out of the car. A physician walking nearby turned, stared at me in astonishment. She blurted, "You must be Gray Temple. Polly's sister is up in room 513, and Polly is staying in room 221 in that motel over yonder."

When I got my mouth back under control, I asked, "How did you know who I was?"

She replied, "You're dressed as a priest, and the tag on the front of your car shows you're from Boone." Only then did I notice that the borrowed car indeed sported a local tag, something my own car lacked. Polly, it seemed, had been worrying aloud to this physician that she'd left town before giving me directions.

For the next two days, coincidence after coincidence pelted us all. Polly's sister's estranged husband returned unannounced to his erstwhile wife's deathbed, asked her forgiveness for a welter of abuses, and the two were reconciled. At one point Polly and I stood on the motel balcony outside her suite, wishing she knew how to contact a cousin in another state with whom she'd lost touch. At that moment the man himself walked across the parking lot in front of us.

Archbishop William Temple (no relation) was once asked his theology of prayer. The one who asked the question braced himself for a lengthy learned answer. The Archbishop replied simply, "When I pray, coincidences happen; when I don't pray, they don't happen."

I wouldn't know how to improve on that answer.

Polly's sister died gently a week later, without discomfort or a lot of medication, surrounded by people who loved her.

· · · · · ·

IT WAS BECOMING CLEAR that God was at work reestablishing a direct relationship with me—and that I had no control whatever over that process except to stay present to it. I tried to think of an initiative I could take to cooperate with what was happening. I settled on signing up for a conference to be held a couple of months later—ironically, at the Kanuga Conference Center in Western North Carolina, the site of the clergy conference I'd fled only a few weeks before.

The conference, entitled "Loaves And Fishes," was being offered by the diocese's Department of Personal Religion, about as loathsome a coven of sappy reactionaries as I could imagine. They didn't much care for me either, and a number of them expressed displeased surprise when I registered. Maybe they suspected sabotage.

Two circumstances led me to apply despite all this. First, the keynoter, Bishop William Folwell, a housebroken Charismatic, was an old conference buddy from other times. I recalled he enjoyed bourbon, so he'd be okay to hang around with. If Bill had been invited to lead the conference, it couldn't be as weird as it looked. And secondly, some of the people who'd be there were among those who had at times spoken of Jesus in my hearing in ways that recalled to me my encounter at Groton.

Jim Radebaugh was on the panel. I figured I could stay out of his way. And Joy wouldn't be with him. I wouldn't be able to stay out of *her* way. She still scared me.

As the time for the conference approached, four events occurred in quick succession that destabilized my paradigm for how the world works. In retrospect I understand that I was being softened up.

My elderly Senior Warden, a dear and wise friend, was taken to the hospital and diagnosed with inoperable cancer. I felt bereft and scared. Soon after, a missionary from Korea, Archer Torrey, happened to be passing through town. I told him how scared and grieved I felt.

· · · · · ·

"Gray, go on a fast for him. Then go anoint him with oil and pray for him so God can heal him," Archer said.

"Archer, I can't heal anybody," I responded.

"Of course you can't heal anybody. But you *can* be the ass Jesus rides into the room on."

I governed my temper, took his advice about the fast, and anointed my friend. He went home well later that week.

I'd like to report that I was delighted and grateful to God. But the fact is, I was even more scared than when he'd first been diagnosed. I was being confronted by something deeply authoritative that I did not understand and was powerless to control.

Then it happened again.

A woman in the church called, asking my help. I was surprised she called because she didn't care for me much—which made it pretty mutual. Now when parents don't like their preacher, you can tell it by how the kids regard the preacher. Her young daughter had always seemed to regard me with a curious loathing. The woman told me that her daughter was in the hospital with something scary. Would I come and visit?

When I arrived I was surprised to see the little girl running around the room apparently healthy and vigorous. No, it turned out, the girl was being slowly poisoned—evidently from some source they could neither identify nor arrest. Lead-based paint? Some toxic household product? It was a mystery. But the trend was accelerating downward. The mother and I had a strained conversation about how puzzling and frightening this all was. I tried to say something consoling, asked her to call me with developments, and rose to go. At the door, an unseen Presence blocked my departure.

"You have not done your job."

I turned around. The mother looked startled. "I haven't done my job," I confessed. "Elizabeth," I said to the daughter who was standing across the room, "Come over here to me." Remarkably, she did so. I took her head in my hands and prayed that Jesus would heal her. Then I left. Nobody stopped me.

The next day I got a phone call from the mother.

Elizabeth was well.

■ ■ ■

As the Loaves and Fishes Conference approached, I was feeling jittery, thinking I had been a fool to sign up for it. One night my fears kept me awake.

I lay in bed dreading the conference and thinking of ways to get out of it. I got to thinking about Kanuga—the conference center where I had spent many, many days and nights over the years. How many ghosts that place held for me—the abortive clergy conference was only the most recent one.

Over the years, Jean and I had gone to a number of training events in human relations at that site. Human Relations Training in T-Groups had been a prominent program in the Episcopal Church since the 1960s. The program combined elements of management training, elements from group psychotherapy, and experimental teaching methods. Strenuous is too mild a term for it. For hours at a time over several days members of a randomly assembled group would thrash around in a bare room trying to figure out what they were there to learn, tempers flaring, terrifying issues of personal acceptability being raked open. The so-called trainers would sit in sphinx-like silence, occasionally intervening to make frustrating critical remarks about how we were doing. Late in the week we'd start detecting the connection between this group and our vestries back home, realizing that what other group members were telling us about ourselves resembled people's reactions to us in more normal settings. We often learned a great deal, but at enormous emotional cost. Each evening we'd spend many hours partying, trying to blow off the tensions and exhilarations we'd felt all day. A number of colleagues, including a seminary classmate of mine, had found T-groups fatally disruptive to their marriages. I understood why. On any number of occasions, in the presence of any number of attractive people, I had resisted the tug into relational chaos. Now here I was, going back to that place wondering if I'd meet God there.

At least, I mused, I'd never betrayed Jean—not literally anyway.

Abruptly I was surrounded by the authoritative Presence. In much less time than it will take for you to read them, four things became instantly clear to me. They reached me in something like this form:

"Gray, it was not for love of me that you did not betray Jean.

"It was not for love of my Law that you did not betray Jean.

"It was not your love for Jean that kept you from betraying her.

"It was your own cowardice in the face of complicated relationships that kept you technically faithful. The outcome of that fear is a good one. But do not confuse cowardice with active virtue."

I was so stunned that I nearly rolled off the bed. I have no idea how long I lay there going back over and over on what I'd been told, admitting and submitting to its truth.

I'd never thought much about *love* for God's Law. But now a verse or two from the Psalter went through my head:

> Blessed is the man that hath not walked in the counsel of the ungodly, nor stood in the way of sinners,* and hath not sat in the seat of the scornful.
>
> But his delight is in the law of the Lord; * and in his law will he exercise himself day and night.(Psalms 1:1–2)

Whatever our critics say about our slackness with the Bible, church-going Episcopalians hear and recite more of it on a given Sunday than the next five denominations combined. That background came through for me that night as those verses bubbled up into my consciousness from so many hours in Groton's chapel.

I lay there realizing that it was, in fact, night—and I was, in fact, exercising myself on God's Law. And it *was* a delight. How? Because I felt the Law as God's generosity to a chaotic human race—the terms for our courteous answering love toward God. Law was *not* a Jewish burden from which Christian grace offered relief. It combined the requirement to be fully human with the gracious power to *be* so. It was God's promise to establish me in personal stability. Right then, meditating on the Law seemed to me to be the third nicest thing you can do in bed.

As sleep finally approached, a thought filled me momentarily:

"I am showing you what it is to be Jew."

■ ■ ■

The town and university where I worked lacked adequate mental health resources. It had a psychiatrist, but people were scared to be seen coming out of his office. There was one public mental health clinic where I served as an ancillary staff member running groups. The university had a psychological service for students as well, and some of the campus ministers worked closely with it. But as somebody said, what were they among so many?

At the time I had what I now understand was an alarmingly large list of people who came to me regularly for a listening ear and an absorbent shoulder. Few of them asked my credentials. In fact, I was not qualified to do what I was attempting.

One night the weight of that responsibility caught up with me. Maybe it was fatigue. And maybe it was God turning up the internal heat, forcing me to scrutinize my life.

After dinner I sat in my chair looking out the window over the town and began musing over the eighteen or so people who were seeking my regular counsel to help them deal with intractable distresses. I was suddenly aware of the sadness of their circumstances and sorrowed that they were not benefiting from wiser assistance than mine. I was startled to find myself weeping—hard.

The last time I'd wept had been on my friend's deck—that had been for me. This time I was at home—it was for other people.

I realized that the Presence had been standing somewhere close behind me for some time. My body had known it before my mind, the hair on my arms standing up. Again, I knew better than to look back.

"You are terribly sad. You are tired. Do you want to come in?"

"In" seemed to mean a warm combination of the Presence, heaven, beatitude, non-specific but wonderfully beckoning.

"I'm grateful to invited," I replied, "but would you take George in first?" George was a counselee.

"I'm pleased with your response. Yes, I will take George. Now would you like to come in?"

"I'd like very much to come in, but would you take Mary beforehand?"

"Thank you for that. Yes, Mary is safe. Now do you want to come in?"

So it went—eighteen times, eighteen invitations, eighteen requests that each counselee be allowed to enter first, eighteen assurances of the counselee's well-being, eighteen responses of pleasure that such was my wish. And then the invitations stopped—before I could reply on my own behalf and say, "I'm ready to come in myself."

I was puzzled that the door was no longer open to me right then. Obviously the Presence knew my puzzlement.

"I am showing you what it is to be a priest."

By the time the Loaves and Fishes Conference began, attending it felt to me like a very bad idea. The chattiest "happy Christian" woman in the region offered me a ride. The drive was only two and a half hours but it felt like months. My right hand clutched the door handle for much of the drive, doubtless expressing my not-so-unconscious desire to leap from the car.

The conference itself was everything I had feared. The first session opened with tacky music—festooned with gratuitous arpeggios—sung and danced to by late-middle-aged adults trying to pretend they were childlike. That's not a sight for the fainthearted. Watching a roomful of paunchy white folks traipsing about the room singing, "They were WALKING and LEAPING and PRAISING GOD!" will put you off your feed. The worship leaders tried to whip us up with encouragements to feel happier than the situation warranted, shouting instructions to find somebody you didn't know and hug them, tell them Jesus loves them and you do too. . . . Brrrr! Even in late November I was sweating with isolated self-consciousness.

Then Bill, the keynoter, stood for his opening address. He seemed poised and serene in his lumberjack shirt, evidently unperturbed by the tackiness of the singing and cavorting. During the course of it he said, "Saul of Tarsus had to be taken to the house of his enemy to be healed." And right then I knew I was in the right place. I muttered, "O God, you got my number all right. I am sure as hell in the house of my enemy."

I must confess that the worship never did much for me that week. Nowadays I can tolerate that type of music and spontaneous dance pretty well, but it's an acquired taste, a slowly acquired taste. During that week, full participation would have cost me more aesthetic breaking and humbling than I could endure right then.

But the spoken presentations got to me. Beginning with Bill, speaker after speaker demonstrated how lucidly intelligible the New Testament becomes once you see that it's describing the effects of being filled with the Holy Spirit. One spoke of how Paul ceases to be seen as a cloying moralist and becomes our enthusiastic encourager once the same Spirit fills us both. Several spoke of the daily task of remaining open to God's Spirit. One spoke of common problems and obstacles to spiritual growth.

The speakers all seemed to share several characteristics. They were affectionately respectful of each other, appreciatively highlighting points made previously by a colleague. They seemed more interested in what they were offering us than in themselves as the deliverers. They could accept correction from each other or from the floor cheerfully, apparently grateful for any gain in overall accuracy.

I felt silent embarrassment to recognize that such humility was rare in the circles I normally moved in.

During discussion periods, the leaders would hesitate briefly as if to pull inside before venturing a reply to a question or comment. A day or so into the conference I was startled to realize that they were probably praying. I'd never seen speakers do that.

With growing admiration of their honesty, I listened more carefully to their content. It was less stupid than I'd been assuming and had its own internal coherence. During question-and-answer periods, I'd often have a notion of what the speaker ought to reply to some inquiry or other. More often than not, the leader would say pretty much what I'd guessed. I realized that I was tracking with them at some level, that we were in the same groove. It felt sort of natural, but I suspected it wasn't entirely.

Each night Bill, the keynoter, and I would meet for conversation; it was always relaxing after the mixed experiences of the day. I described to him the circumstances leading me to the conference, the spiritual jam-up, failures at prayers, and the unanticipated buffetings from God. He didn't make much comment at the time.

But on the eve of the conference's close, Bill asked me to his room to meet with a few other people. I was dismayed when I saw who they were.

· · · · · ·

One was a lapsed parishioner of mine whom I'd avoided all week. The other was a young woman Jean and I had mentored when she was an undergraduate, inculcating reliably radical political views and T-group leadership skills. But she had gone to North Carolina State College for grad school where she had joined a campus religious group and succumbed to Pentecostalism. I regarded that as tantamount to a prefrontal lobotomy, and had missed no occasion since then to tell her so, in public and in private.

Neither of these folks appeared any happier to see me than I was to see them. We watched each other warily until Bill broke into the silence:

"Each of you has spoken to me privately this week. You've each admitted that you're lonely. You've each acknowledged that you live fairly close to the other two. You've also each told me you can't stand the other two. If you guys could get it together and get reconciled, you might be able to start something back home that would keep your spirits up."

All three of us sucked wind.

■ ■ ■

I don't know how Bill managed to stay so calm after tossing that bomb into the room. Alice and Helen looked wide-eyed and nostril-flared, like deer staring into headlights—I bet I didn't look much different. None of that fazed Bill. He levelly challenged each of us to tell each other what we'd been telling him about each other. It was agony. Not for the first time that week, I was struck by how much you can sweat in November.

But we did as he said. We started talking to each other straight. Alice and I discussed the grudge, left over from an unfruitful counseling series, that had led her to leave my congregation. We realized we wanted it behind us. Helen and Alice worked on their grudge (which I didn't pay much attention to) while I caught my breath from my go-round with Alice.

Then Helen rounded on me: "Gray, pretending like I'm still your friend is costing me more than it gains me. I'm sick of it. You take every occasion to humiliate me publicly. You say it's your opposition to Fundamentalism. But I'm no Fundamentalist and you damn well know it. You're dry as a bone spiritually—and it shows. You're just mad at me that I'm not dry right now. I've had it with you, buddy."

And God gave me uncharacteristic grace at that moment to listen without interrupting or arguing. I think that's the first time in my life I ever felt compelled to agree with a critic. I heard myself replying, "I agree with everything you've said. I don't blame you for dropping our friendship. I *have* been arid. Being around you makes me jealous, just like you said. It embarrasses me too because I'm supposed to know more than you do—but I don't think I know as much. During this conference I've seen the integrity of your position. I don't expect to ever like the sort of music you guys seem to like, and I doubt if I'll ever feel real warm or fuzzy, but I'm clear that you've been right and I've been wrong. So I'm making you a promise. From now on, whenever people like me are making things hard on people like you, I'm gong to cross the room and stand with you all."

It was the best I could offer right then and I think it was enough for God to use. Within minutes, I became aware of the Presence of Jesus in the room. It was like the time at boarding school when Jesus came into my cubicle as a light, though there was nothing visual about my awareness, only a sense of a person being there. But the air seemed like it was filled with helium—it made our voices higher and faster, filling us with the impulse to laugh happily.

When our disputes were composed, Bill dropped to his knees. He asked Helen to pray over him, using glossalalia. She did so—and I understood what she'd said! This was my first exposure to someone speaking or praying in tongues, and it startled me to have it seem natural. When I reported my interpretation of Helen's prayer to him, he jumped with surprise. My words seemed non-specific to me, but something in them grabbed him personally . . . without the others knowing it. So I dropped to my knees and asked Helen to do the same thing for me.

She did.

Bill understood it.

. . . . . .

He reported to me that Jesus was entering me with some badly needed soothing gentleness—sopping up a lot of rage I'd been plagued with over recent years—promising that my life would come to be a continual *Te Deum Laudamus*. (The latter is a chant Episcopalians sometime use in worship. Bill couldn't have known that it's my favorite bit in our Prayer Book.) The message was clear and directed at me personally.

At the closing Eucharist the next morning, I was among several priests asked to hear sacramental confessions. I was surprised that the most difficult element for me—that of offering counsel and a penance—felt effortless for the first time. I realized that the Spirit was doing the ministry through me and my role was to relax and let it flow.

After the service I spoke to my own bishop who was at the conference. I told him I'd had a fresh conversion and needed his advice. He referred me to Jim Radebaugh as a spiritual director—the man whose wife had jump-started this whole process months earlier when she confronted me at the clergy conference. The bishop obviously appreciated Jim as I could not have right then, discerning in him the inexhaustible patience that accompanies spiritual maturity—just the right man to coach a spiritual upstart like myself. I was in no mood to argue. I sought Jim out and was startled at how graciously he agreed.

Over the years Jim's (and Joy's) friendship proved enormously fruitful. I cannot count the number of times that a phone call to Jim alleviated the confusion or depression that can sometimes overtake me. Occasionally a routine phone call prompted an unplanned visit after Jim discerned, from a question or a random bit of information, some issue that deserved more attention than I'd known to give it. This happened once after I casually described the inexplicable behavior of a parishioner. Where I saw eccentricity, Jim saw the interface between spirituality and mental illness.

I rode home with the same chatty woman—who once again talked the entire drive without pausing to draw breath. Her talk suited me just fine. Hell, *she* suited me just fine.

Jeez—I really *am* getting gentle! I mused.

. . . . .

Jean

. . . . . .

I ARRIVED HOME feeling peaceful and joyous. I was happy to see Jean—happier than she was to see me, as it turned out.

Helen and Alice burst into the house minutes behind me to tell Jean what a great time it had been, trying both to share and to prolong the experience we'd just had.

Eventually Jean managed to chill them out of the house. I guess it *was* a bit of a stretch for Jean to have to listen to two bubbly friends, obviously real snug with her husband, cooing about a delicious experience they'd shared apart from her.

I'm not the most intuitive husband around, but that did seem like a good occasion to put in some one-on-one time with Jean. We sat down together and I tried to relate what had happened to me. I recall being pretty calm about it, but that's not how she remembers it.

About half-an-hour into my recitation, I asked if there were any beer in the house.

"Thank God!" she muttered.

"Thank God for what?" I asked.

"At least you're not a *complete* saint yet!"

I let the jab pass—with unintentionally infuriating placidity.

After dinner a group of students came over for a long-scheduled meeting. I was enjoying myself. They were discussing some of their religious questions and I was struck with how they hung on some of my observations, observations that again felt personally effortless. I became aware of how much easier it is to do this sort of thing when I quit trying to be clever and let God take charge.

A couple of students lingered after the meeting, but our amicable conversation screeched to an abrupt halt when Jean came rushing down the hall toward the living room. Her robe flapping, hair flying like a banshee's, Jean bellowed for them to get out of her house right then, that she hadn't seen her husband for better than a week and she'd be damned if she

. . . . . .

was going to wait for a bunch of self-absorbed students to clear out on their own.

They scattered. I followed her down the hall to our bedroom.

Then she rounded on me. Her resentment poured out and out. Normally I'd be pretty defensive in the face of such anger, especially coming at me from one who is naturally gracious. This time I simply prayed—*real* silently.

"Lord, this isn't going like I'd have expected. What do you want me to do?"

"Keep out of this. Don't reply. Do not take any of this personally. This is not your fight."

So I kept quiet and listened. At length I heard Jean take another tack. "I think I'm afraid I'm losing you. I think I'm afraid you won't need me. You've gone someplace I can't get to."

I'm not a good evangelist and was no more adept at "leading a person to Christ" then than I am today. God, on the other hand, *is* good at it, so I said to Jean, "I didn't ask to get to this state, although I'm real glad to be here. I don't know how to tell somebody how to get here—and that scares me because I want you with me. But I bet if you asked God about it, something would happen." Then I wisely shut up.

Jean was sitting on the bed, her back to the pillows against the headboard. She said something like, "God, I'm lonesome and scared. You've done something with Gray I don't know anything about. Please help me."

She gave a momentary convulsive heave as though vomiting or burping. Then she gazed past the foot of the bed at something I couldn't see, and a smile took her over. She later told me it was a personal light and that sounded pretty familiar.

Since then I've talked to any number of others who got converted at different times from the people they were married to. In comparison, I think Jean and I had it remarkably easy. We got to step across the stream where it's narrow.

WHAT HAD HAPPENED to me at the conference and afterwards goes by a number of names, depending on what faith community you're in. The people who offered the Loaves and Fishes Conference were "Charismatics," so they called it "Baptism in the Holy Spirit." "Baptism" comes from a Greek word meaning "to soak." Spirit-baptism is Jesus' own term (cf. Acts 1:5) for soaking in the vitality of God.

Spirit-baptism is characteristic of the Pentecostal denominations that began proliferating in the United States and around the world beginning in 1901. These people came from the Holiness denominations, a nineteenth century outgrowth of Methodist revivalism. When they tried to make sense of their new sensory awareness of God's immanence, they were unlikely to consult anybody as orthodox as Bernard of Clairvaux or John of the Cross. They relied on the Bible because it was all they had, knew, or trusted. Using their Bibles and their own experiences, these people worked out detailed understandings of what theologians call Ascetical Theology, the study of the soul's relationship to God, emphasizing helpful spiritual disciplines and practices. The Pentecostals (the white ones, at least; black Pentecostals have always been more radical) were religiously, politically, and socially quite conservative. As Pentecostalism made its way into the "mainline denominations," becoming the "Charismatic Movement," conservatism came with it. The average Charismatic today is a politically conservative Fundamentalist—even if she happens to be Presbyterian or Roman Catholic.

I wasn't. When I fell into Spirit-baptism I was an ultraliberal-pacifist-theological-existentialist; I emerged an ultraliberal-pacifist-theological-existentialist who actively loved Jesus.

Over the years I've been grateful and surprised at how little of that God seems to want me to change. (I discovered that the experience of Spirit-baptism has no manifest theological content and is not under patent to the right wing.) What has changed is that I no longer have permission whatever to despise people who hold other opinions—a discomfiting handicap for a temperament like mine.

Now one thing that characterizes Spirit-baptism is the ability to pray in syllables that the speaker does not personally understand—glossalalia, or, more commonly, "speaking in tongues." In fact, some Pentecostal groups insist that you aren't truly Spirit-baptized unless you display this gift, so there is some status anxiety, some self-doubt attached to the whole issue of whether or not you can pray in tongues.

Feeling that self-doubt, I wanted that gift.

I asked for it.

It didn't happen.

So I got Helen and Alice to pray for me to get it. There was no sense in asking Jean to pray for it, because she didn't do it either and she lacked my urgency about it. Helen and Alice prayed over me like the 450 priests of Baal on Mount Carmel—with the same outcome: zilch. So I tried some emotional ploys, trying to get God to soften up.

I got self-pitying. No result.

I got scornful of people who did it. No result.

I decided it was only for conservatives, not for cool liberals. No result.

Eventually I became resigned. I'd just have to love God humbly, without that gift.

One day, a month or so after the Loaves and Fishes Conference, a phone call came from the distraught husband of a parishioner. Mary Lou was in the hospital. They'd operated and found a cancer beyond repair. A private, self-contained woman, she hadn't wanted anyone to know she might have cancer, so this was the first I'd heard of her illness.

Helen was in town at the time. She knew Mary Lou and asked to come to the hospital with me. In fact, as I recall, she drove.

On our way, I was lamenting not having so strong a faith as others I knew, wishing I had more to share with Mary Lou. As I imagined standing by her bed and simply allowing the love of God to flow into her without my filtration, I discovered that I was whispering in syllables I couldn't understand—and I was aware of a wonderful personal warmth as I did so.

Tongues—glossalalia—there it was. Once it was for somebody else, I guess I could relax enough to receive it.

Helen and I stood by Mary Lou's bed. She was brave and composed in a tight-lipped way. I was impelled to ask her if she would risk receiving God's love. She replied that it indeed felt risky getting her hopes up, that the coming weeks would be difficult enough without having to cope with disappointment. I prayed silently for some instructions.

"Ask her what is most immediately painful."

"Mary Lou, is there anything that is especially painful right this minute?"

"Well, yes," she replied. "My neck is painfully stiff."

With her permission, I asked God to relieve the pain in her neck. The next day she reported that her neck had improved quickly.

"Ask what's most painful now."

Her incision was painful—she had developed an infection. We prayed about that.

The next day her incision was no longer infected or painful. I asked what we might ask God for today. She wanted to be well from the surgery soon enough to be able to go home for Christmas and perhaps make the cruise she and her husband had been planning to take after the holiday. So we prayed she'd go home soon—and our next visit was at her house. She wanted to be well enough for the cruise. We prayed for it. She was.

When Mary Lou returned from the cruise, we had another talk. It was clear to her by now that all the small prayers we'd offered had been granted. We spoke of how God was offering her the knowledge that she was precious in small, digestible bits. Was she ready to ask for the big one? She was. We prayed for the cancer to leave her. During the course of that prayer, she gently surrendered herself to Jesus and offered herself to be his own.

Mary Lou's cancer went into remission. Her personality changed in subtle ways as well.

Her diffident air remained, but her crippling shyness was gone, replaced by a merry, incisive, yet deeply kind, wit.

Jean and I moved to St. Patrick's in the Diocese of Atlanta, and gradually lost touch with her.

Six years later the cancer returned. Mutual friends called to tell me she had died. It was at least a six-hour drive back to Boone. I arrived in town half an hour late for her funeral.

As a number of friends told me, she ended her days at the hospital surrounded by friends and family. She was sitting up in the bed, choosing hymns for them to sing together. If someone objected to one of her selections, she'd reply, "I'm the one dying, I get to choose." Somewhere in the course of that hymn-sing Mary Lou slipped away, retaining the smile she'd worn for the last six years.

. . . . . .

PREACHING IS A LOT EASIER and more fun after you're Spirit-baptized. Trusting that Jesus wants to make his thoughts available to other people through you makes sermon preparation a matter of prayerful discussion rather than isolated brain-wracking.

I was just moving into that fresh discovery one week when I was looking over the prescribed readings for the upcoming Sunday. The gospel reading contained a reference to Satan.

Those of us whose theologies lean towards liberalism are chary of talk about the devil. We tend to read references to Old Scratch and his attendant demons as figurative at best. Those of us who believe the gospel entails clear social and political implications view the devil as an avatar of an outmoded, repressive, socio-political consciousness. But I found I'd been naive.

Here's how it happened.

The Saturday morning before I was to preach on the verses referring to the devil:

> You are from your father the devil, and you choose to do your father's
> desires. He was a murderer from the beginning and does not stand in
> the truth, because there is no truth in him. When he lies, he speaks
> according to his own nature, for he is a liar and the father of lies.
> (John 8:44)

I was standing in my bedroom, musing on the passage, frustrated that I didn't really understand the reference. It hit me that nowadays I could put such a question to Jesus directly, confident that I would get an answer. So, without giving the consequences much thought, I asked Jesus, "What is the devil stuff really about?"

As usual, a whole lot happened nearly at once.

I felt myself being coated with the love of God—as though warm oil were being poured all over me, and as though I were being embraced from behind. But almost simultaneously the very air in front of me seemed to split open like a curtain, revealing an appalling pitch-dark void. As I looked into it, I realized that something alive lurked inside. It was like entering a cave and sensing a malignant reptilian presence stirring just out of sight. But the malignancy at the bottom of this pit was vast—larger than the very solar system—and filled with a seething hatred that resembles nothing I have experienced on earth.

I sensed some things about it—I'm not sure how. That impotent raging hatred is aimed at God. You and I are of little interest to it—except in that in harming us it might discomfit God.

The sight knocked me backwards, leaving me sprawled across the bed. My initial reaction was abject terror, like a rabbit cornered by a wildcat. But I managed to plunge through the bottom of my terror and discovered a profounder *sadness* than I'd ever known. It broke my heart that a universe as lovely as ours should contain something so utterly loathsome, so inimical to all beauty.

I spoke to Jesus again, groping to articulate the insight he'd given me. "When you died on the Cross, it was to break the power of *that*—it was to hurl yourself into that pit, to dare it to take its best shot at you—right?"

"Yes."

"When you died 'for our sins' you were really looking over our shoulders at *that*, weren't you?"

"Yes."

For what it's worth, the Ransom Theory of the Atonement—the notion that on the Cross Jesus overcame the devil's power and broke his grip on us—has made deep sense to me at an instinctive level ever since then. Similarly, conventional "substitutionary" theories—

that Jesus took our punishment for us, punishment that either God's arrangements of justice or God's annoyance at us make necessary—have seemed to me relatively impertinent. A Cross which addresses only human sin today seems less cogent, and, if truth be known, somewhat trivial.

There is vastly more at stake on the Cross than my little badness—or yours.

I WAS LATE TO A COMMITTEE MEETING in a town eighty mountain miles from my house. It began at ten, about the time I started out. I arrived just after the committee sat down for lunch. As luck would have it, the only vacant seat was beside the chairman. I rushed into the dining room in exaggerated haste and threw myself into the empty seat.

"Forgive me for being late," I requested.

"Oh, that's okay," replied the chairman. "We hadn't got much done so far."

An astute observer seated across the table from me remarked, "Gray, did you notice he didn't really forgive you?"

An awkward silence ensued as each of us ruminated on the truth of that observation—and the tackiness of being confronted with it.

After a few moments I remarked, "Yeah, I guess he didn't forgive me really. Uh, Jim—would you really forgive me for being late?"

Jim laughed nervously and said, "I guess I didn't. Yes, I do forgive you for being late."

I don't recall that a lot more was said. I was in a brown study, musing over what had just taken place.

On the drive home I was preoccupied with the episode. Why had it gotten under my skin? Did it really matter that Jim hadn't initially forgiven me? Oddly, it felt like it mattered. How did our observer know to tag it? What *is* forgiveness, anyway? I realized I wasn't sure. What did I know about it? I couldn't think of much. Did I ever forgive other people? Not that I could recall immediately. Had I ever received forgiveness? Hard to remember. Had I ever preached on it? No—in fact I'd always avoided the topic, come to think of it. Had I ever heard a sermon on it? Not that I could recall. Could I describe or define forgiveness? Not easily, I realized. My attempts all pointed to forgiveness being some sort of contrivance.

When I got home I asked Jean to sit with me. I told her about the episode and opened

· · · · · ·

my ignorance of the topic to her. She acknowledged that though the topic wasn't one that preoccupied her, she really didn't know much more than I did. As we talked, the conversation started to feel unpleasant for both of us. We were working hard not to mention that in seven years of marriage, we'd stockpiled a fair amount of unforgiveness between us. Now it sat in the living room like the proverbial elephant. There was only the way forward—no way back.

We sucked in a deep breath, said, "Shall we?" and prayed. We asked Jesus to open this topic to us, and then resolved to revisit it in conversation until we felt a better grasp on it.

■ ■ ■

Over the course of the next couple of weeks some understandings of forgiveness fell into place for both of us.

Jean and I discussed various forms of counterfeit forgiveness. For example, to say, "It didn't matter," is a subtle way of saying, "You're inconsequential." To say, "No problem," is dismissive. To say, "You couldn't help it," is synonymous with, "You're pathetic."

Various passages in the New Testament showed us that Jesus' teachings on forgiveness are formulated as commands, not descriptive statements. Assuming that Jesus wouldn't command us to do something beyond our ability, we reasoned that forgiveness must lie within the reach of our wills. It's something we can decide to do.

That cleared up some confusion right there. One reason I'd never preached on it had to do with assuming that forgiveness means magically feeling good about somebody I really feel bad about. That would be tantamount to assuming that Jesus requires that we be phony. That no longer squared with the one we were coming to know.

If forgiveness is something we exercise with our wills over against our feelings, what do we actually *do* with our wills? What are the decisions required?

Here Jean's graduate studies in psychotherapy guided us. Forgiving another person had to begin with a frank reckoning of the damage the other party's behavior had done us. We had to say an honest "Ouch!" We had to drop the self-protective posture that insists I'm too big and tough to be affected by some inconsequential little twerp. Admitting hurt feels risky and painful. No wonder it requires a conscious resolution.

The second decision is based on the Old and New Testaments: we are to renounce revenge. All over the place in the Bible we read, "Vengeance is mine, I will repay," where God is the speaker. Jesus commands us to say something like, "Even though any human court in the world would call it justifiable homicide if I killed my enemy, for your sake I won't take the shot if he walks in front of my cross-hairs."

Episcopalians learn to confess sins "in thought, word, and deed." That's a good checklist. Renouncing vengeful deeds may be no fun, but at least it's clear. You drop lawsuits. You quit letting air out of your enemy's tires. But lots of times revenge is more subtle, harder to catch yourself at.

What about vengeful words? Is praying openly for someone to receive insight into their own character and motives vengeful? I think so. Is a knowing silent smile when my enemy is mentioned a vengeful communication? What do you think?

And then we get to the really hard part—renouncing vengeful thoughts. Much of my time alone in a car gets spent concocting revenge fantasies. I need to promise God I'll try not to do that—and when I catch myself doing it anyway, pray to be forgiven, and then pray for the person I'm mad at.

I can tell when I'm getting somewhere with renouncing revenge—it feels like it's killing me. It's as bad as deciding to admit I got hurt, as bad as saying "Ouch!"

The third decision has to do with myself, with knowing so much about the splinters in my brother's eye and so little about the two-by-fours in my own. To put it in Jean's professional parlance, I renounce secondary benefits from the injury I've sustained. I promise not to use my enemy's behavior as the excuse for my own misbehavior or even for my self-pity. If I decide to be bad, that's on my record, not his.

Again, you can tell when you're doing this right—it hurts real bad to promise all that.

The fourth decision grows out of Jesus' hideous command that we bless those who curse us, that we pray for those who use us badly. In effect, I tell God that if I notice my enemy being blessed, I won't mess it up with my voodoo. "If I see my enemy driving down my street in a new BMW, honking her horn and grinning like a possum, I'll know you've answered my prayer for her."

Guess how that one feels? That's how you know you're doing it right.

■ ■ ■

When any of us has offered God those four decisions, we are not likely to feel awash with the peace of God. At first we're more likely to feel resentment, experiencing the unfairness of being injured then being told to pray for the blessing of the guilty.

But you need to peer beneath resentment, where you'll find a new place for a sense of vulnerability. Unforgiveness is a sort of burglar alarm, poised to alert us to the possibility of further harm from the person we're mad at—and eventually from anyone who resembles her. I keep myself bitter in order to keep safe. And God is asking me to be unsafe again.

Up to this point Jean and I were concentrating on decisions we have to make. But past this point we have to ask God to do things for us that we can't do for ourselves. The fifth step in forgiving another person is asking God to makes some changes inside us.

First, I acknowledge that without God's protection, my enemy can readily injure me again. So, "God, keep me safe," is my prayer.

Then I ask God to show me why my enemy got created. I've found it helpful is to ask why God delights in my enemy. "God, why did you make this person in the first place? What delights you about them? Show me your own pleasure in this person so I can try to agree with it."

Remarkably delightful stuff about my enemy often breaks into my awareness. This man who's such a blow-hard is in fact very loyal to his friends; I might consider becoming one of those friends. This apparently selfish woman has a passionate concern for children; the community is better off for her being here. As I see someone's virtues, my inner rage gets quieter.

Finally I ask God the biggest favor of all: to heal my heart towards the one who hurt me—and towards everyone that by now reminds me of them.

People say you can't prove the existence of God. But I believe there is a very simple way to prove God's existence. To do so you simply forgive someone who has hurt you because Jesus asks you to. Then you ask God to heal your heart. If your heart gets soothed after a reasonable period of that prayer, you've proved the existence of God. If there is no change in you, if you still feel bitter and reserved around your enemy after obeying God's requirement, you've essentially proved God does not exist. You can sleep late on Sunday morning guilt-free and you can quit tithing.

There are one or two caveats that will occur to any grown-up trying to forgive another person. It's difficult but important to recognize that forgiveness is primarily a transaction between us and God, not between us and the former enemy.

Forgiving another person does not necessarily imply that they acted wrongly—it simply means that pain was exchanged.

And forgiveness needs to quit being a wrenching, specific act and become both a habitual reflex and a way of living with other people. Jesus was a realist about the necessity of repeating forgiveness—seventy times seven. I must be a realist as well. My forgiving you does not change you—only my bearing towards you.

For all its pain, forgiveness is just about the most nourishing spiritual exercise you can undertake. If you wanted to jump-start your own sense of God's presence, you could do far worse than learning to forgive someone who has harmed you. It is a Christ-like action, taking onto yourself the impact of another's sin, going to your own Cross on their behalf. When you're not only doing what Jesus *commands*, but also doing what Jesus *does*, it's not difficult to sense his companionship.

. . . . . .

CHURCHES THAT GO FOR the Charismatic Renewal share all the difficulties any congregation suffers—and then some. For example, Charismatic air-conditioning systems break down at about the same rate as traditionalist air conditioners—but in a traditional Episcopal parish nobody tells the rector that it's God's judgment. In the long run it's all worth it, I think, but it's not for sissies.

At St. Patrick's, the one thing we've never had any serious conflicts about is our Charismatic identity. My predecessor had wisely begun his work with the vestry and the leadership core of the congregation, from there it had gently radiated outward during his remaining tenure.

Rather, the conflicts that surfaced shortly after my arrival had to do with what *flavor* of Charismatic we were going to represent. That took me by surprise, to say the least. The root system of the conflict pattern should have been simple to detect: it was a standard old member/new member turf battle. But I missed seeing it for a long time. Here's how it happened.

My predecessor had taken a group of traditional lifelong Episcopalians and introduced them to the personal power of God. Word spread through the city that there was an Episcopal church in north Atlanta hospitable to people who had been Spirit-baptized. This had enormous appeal to people who felt estranged from their previous congregations once the power of God hit them.

Why were they estranged? Because Spirit-baptism turns a low-maintenance churchgoer into a high-maintenance church member. In your car, it would be like popping the clutch—leaving a trail of rubber on the street behind you. Consequently we survival-oriented clergy tend to see the Charismatic Movement as perhaps not as bad as, say, AIDS—but definitely not as good as, say, flu. A fresh sense of God's presence that excited these lay people had met with a chilly reception from their clergy and fellow parishioners. So they'd dropped out of the Episcopal Church, often after stormy confrontations with the clergy and their erstwhile fellow parishioners.

Many of them wound up in neighborhood Bible studies led by the enthusiastic but untrained. Some fetched up in denominations that viewed Spirit-baptism favorably, but attached it to biblical fundamentalism and political conservatism. Most of them continued to miss the sacraments.

So there had been an influx of returning ex-Episcopalians to St. Patrick's. My predecessor had skillfully managed to integrate these newcomers into parish life. But between my predecessor's departure and my arrival nobody understood how important it was to continue to attend to that task. Naturally as a newcomer myself I didn't know who was who and which was which. And it took a long time to get a handle on the seething resentments and reciprocal judgments that were sloshing around our otherwise merry parish.

Long-term members still regarded much of the ministry as the clergy's job; the newcomers regarded themselves as ministers. Long-term members had been through confirmation classes that stressed Scripture, Reason, and Tradition as the tripartite norm for belief and behavior. Newcomers relied on the Bible and were suspicious of appeals to Tradition or Reason. Long-term members thought worship ought to be done "decently and in order" (1 Corinthians 14:40), a passage much loved of Episcopalians and Presbyterians. Newer members found that stodgy.

I contributed to the growing tension—by simply failing to bring to bear a lot of things I'd learned "back before I was saved." Stuff like group dynamics and organization development. I was trying to demonstrate to my new congregation how spiritual I was, and was reluctant to appear "worldly." That wasted a lot of time—and was inauthentic to boot.

A couple of years into my ministry at St. Patrick's, I was utterly miserable. I contemplated running away to join the circus—following the elephants with shovel and bucket seemed clean work in comparison to my own.

One night I was seated on the hearth in front the fireplace. I was in despair. I prayed to God real hard and urgently to get me out of this mess, to take me somewhere else.

Suddenly Jesus was there—not visually, but unmistakably. This time he was in front of me.

"Are you through? Have you said everything you need?"

"Yessir," I stammered.

Jesus then momentarily opened a vision to me, a vision of a thoroughly righteous community of worshipers and servants of God. These people were emotionally honest. They disagreed with each other strongly and often, but without acrimony or overpersonalization. They had a high tolerance for paradox. They spoke the truth. They could admit when they didn't know something without having to fake it. They delighted in each other. They rejected us/them polarities, embracing people different from themselves.

"Do you like what you see?"

"That is perfectly glorious!" I replied.

"The way to that community passes through what you're experiencing now."

"Why does it have to be that way?" I asked.

"Because they are a petty little people right now—and you are a petty little priest. You must all get heartily sick of operating this way."

"If we go through this present nasty period, will it lead to that?"

"Yes. If you ask me to relieve what's happening to you right now, it will lead to a different outcome—not necessarily worse, but different. The anguish you are going through presently is the necessary way to the community I'm showing you."

"I want that community more than anything I've ever seen. So double the misery . . . triple it," I replied. "That kind of community is cheap at any price!"

The moment the visit was over anxiety and resentment washed over me once more. I was as miserable as I'd been a few minutes before. And I stayed that way for a long time. In fact, elements of that conflict pattern—alongside a whole lot of fun and excitement—smoldered beneath the surface of St. Patrick's for the next fifteen years. And Jesus—or we—did indeed double it and triple it over and over again.

What had changed was this: I could no longer forget that I'd chosen to live in the middle those conflicts. From now on, the pains and terrors of rectorship in that parish were finally the fruit of answered prayer.

. . . . .

A Cleansing

· · · · · ·

SEVERAL MEMBERS OF ST. PATRICK'S, including me, became interested in the application of the church's ministry of healing to emotional pains. Pioneered by Agnes Sanford, a noted practitioner of healing through prayer, "healing of memories" had strong cachet among Charismatic Episcopalians. A training organization operated by Anne White of Florida, an exponent of Agnes' ministry, seemed a convenient opening for our plunge. I had become pretty used to putting up with the fundamentalism and political conservatism that increasingly characterized all things Charismatic, so I figured I could tolerate the training event.

The training involved lecture, discussion, and journaling, in addition to undergoing the "healing of memories" procedure. The actual healing procedure entailed a three-hour session with two trained ministers who would lead me through a life-confession and various forms of prayer for pardon, release, and inner healing. That was fine with me—I had amassed a sufficient store of emotional woes to suspect I could benefit from the experience.

But as my time approached, I grew tenser—and the tension gathered around a single issue: my work as a referral agent to abortion clinics while a college chaplain. In that largely fundamentalist milieu I knew I was headed for trouble.

Not all of the trouble was external—much of it resided in me, unconfronted. Everyone connected with the abortion process is painfully aware of the wracking ambivalence that roils in its wake. Though in a fallen world, abortion is sometimes the least terrible of several sorry choices, it is never morally or psychologically antiseptic. Our present cultural climate, which insists on oversimplifying complex issues in "either/or" terms, prevents the level of public discussion the issue deserves. No matter which side we claim, we are always either with people who agree with us, trying to sturdy each other up, or we're defending ourselves against opponents who despise us. Such a milieu produces no clarity at all.

As a college chaplain, I was one of two clergy to whom the campus physician would refer students to when their pregnancy tests came back positive. They would stagger into my office in shock, snuffling, "The doc said you might be able to help me—you see, I'm . . . I'm. . . ."

And I'd take it from there. We would carefully discuss her options, weighing the pros and cons of each. Almost invariably the woman would choose abortion. My job then was to acquaint her with the safest facilities and warn her against all the unsafe expedients. I would always offer follow-up discussions. She would always agree—then, predictably, never show up, ducking my eye on campus when we'd pass.

Over the course of seven years I had been involved in several hundred such conversations.

Leaving campus ministry was sad for me, but I knew I would not miss that aspect of it. Afterward, maybe because I was so relieved to be out of it, I never faced into my accumulated feelings.

Now doubts, regrets, a sense of contamination, and the fatigue most people involved in abortion have to combat, caught up with me. I was about to spend three hours in intense, prayerful conversation with a team of ministers who would sift through my life.

The team leader assigned to me was a Roman Catholic Benedictine monk.

The night before I barely slept. I felt great pressure to be quit of this issue, to be scrubbed, to abandon the pain of my previous involvement and sink into the comforting moral certainty of the opposite position. But to do it in front of a Roman priest/monk? If he went in for penances, I'd be saying "Hail Marys" until the cows came home.

So I prayed. "Lord, what do you want me to do with that issue tomorrow? Should I bring it up?"

"I want you to bring it up and pay close attention to the monk's counsel. I will be using his voice."

That settled that.

The following day I went into a small private room with the monk and a woman trainee who would to assist him. He asked if there were any matters burdening my conscience. It took me a long time to get the words out.

"I was an abortion counselor for several years. I am implicated in the murders of several hundred children." Hyperbolic, I know, but that's how it tumbled out.

He paused a long time and looked at me steadily. His assistant stared at me aghast. Then he spoke gently: "You are nothing of the sort. You are not a murderer. You are not that wicked, nor are you that passionate. In any event, my church notwithstanding, the moral status of abortion is not as neat and clear as murder. So the sin of murder is not what you need to confess. What you need to confess is this: in several hundred instances, you were God's representative, and God had a will, and you did not once ask what God's will was."

It took me a while to recover from that simple truth. When I could pay attention again, he gently absolved me.

Back in my room, I told the Lord I understood why I had to open the matter to that monk. I thanked him for pressing me, and acknowledged that the monk's counsel was his own.

It struck me later that I was still mired in the ambiguity of the issue. But I don't think Jesus traffics in oversimplifications.

· · · · · ·

IN SEMINARY we'd been taught that clergy and vestries are natural enemies. Of course, our teachers didn't know they were teaching that. It was the involuntary shudder that accompanied each mention of some professor's past life in the parish. If we'd been a high church place, they would have crossed themselves.

Anytime some editor wants to put together a book called *Vestry Horror Stories For Midnight Reading*, put him in touch with me—I can supply some of the best. But I could as easily fill a collection featuring *Vestry Heroics*, perhaps even *Vestry Sainthood*. It is my settled opinion that the vestry meeting can be the best setting for the mature exercise of the Gifts of the Spirit (1 Corinthians 12:7–12). I've seen it many times over the years. A member will speak, and we know we're hearing Wisdom. Another will reflect on the will of God in some situation, and when she's finished, the stillness in the room tells us that we've just heard Prophecy. Good stuff happens when a vestry prays for someone's healing.

The trick lies in teaching vestry members to pray as a group.

That really is possible once you understand why people get on vestries in the first place. It's not always just because their wives insisted it was their turn. People (including vestry-folk) frequent churches with the forlorn hope that they might actually encounter God. That's hardly the only reason they're there, and it's so basic nobody talks about it much. But whatever else they're doing in church and eventually on a vestry, they're listening for "a rumor of angels."

Once I realized that my vestry needed to become a prayer-based community, I had to find a way to invite them into it. I would have to press against their reluctance to pray together. I eventually learned to overcome vestry resistance to prayer by paying attention to my own. Why don't *I* like to pray extemporaneously in a small group? Well, there's the risk of the leader manipulating the prayer's direction, that's bruising when I have bared my soul.

. . . . . .

Then there's my fear of being crowded into inauthentic behavior, of having to contrive unfelt emotions. And suppose if folks do get to praying without books and I wasn't very good at it? Furthermore, suppose everyone else is having a grand time with God, and I can't hear or feel anything? I'd be exposed as a spiritual imposter. Too risky. Far safer to read one of the services out of the Book of Common Prayer; you don't have to be very "spiritual" to do that.

So I'd have to find a means for us to address God together that would protect each member from bullying, that required no display of spiritual virtuosity or pyrotechnics, and that made place for people who were having a bad day. It had to lie within the abilities of everyone in the room.

My initial attempts with the vestry at St. Patrick's were only partially successful. All of us agreed to the principle, but the actual execution remained problematic. Happily, one vestry member returned from a conference with just the spark we needed. He demonstrated its ease by teaching us all quickly and gracefully how to pray freely together—about practical concerns as well as spiritual ones.

The method he taught us was simple. When the vestry has a decision to make, the leader (it could be the rector, the warden, or a volunteer) asks everyone to put the decision to the side and remain silent for five minutes. During the silence people imagine Jesus in the room and pay attention to how that Presence looks, feels, or sounds. If someone prefers not to try that, they are asked simply to pray for the others—no skill required for that. Following the silence, the leader asks each person to report briefly on the experience.

We amazed ourselves. A vestry member would typically say something like, "He stood behind Marge saying, 'Pay attention to what she says.'" That will usually jar Marge, because she thought her perception was too weird to share, but now maybe she'd better. Or someone will say, "I just prayed for the rest of you." Another might say, "I sense that he's happier about this situation than we are." And so on. Much more often than not, when everyone in the circle has spoken, the elements of the decision are in place—and some members will gently have altered their original positions without coercion.

We had been praying this way for several years when my vestry and I went on retreat to resolve a sticky financial decision, the collision of two mutually opposed good ideas. I wanted the vestry to raise $250,000 to underwrite a new translation of the Bible into colloquial Swahili for use in East Africa where Jean and I had been missionaries. The vestry insisted that the God-given purpose statement we'd recently been excited about directed our outreach expenditures closer to our own city.

We debated it strenuously. I was in it up to my armpits, quite certain about what was right, smoldering with infrared annoyance that no one else could see it the way I did.

Someone suggested prayer. I'd have looked like a pagan if I'd said no so I could keep arguing, so I reluctantly joined the silence.

I growled silent displeasure to Jesus at the position the others were taking. I knew it wasn't what I was supposed to be doing, but I was too worked up to do anything else.

Even without my really taking part, the prayer worked anyway:

"Their freedom, stretched over time, is the canvas on which I paint my art."

"Well, since you put it *that* way . . . ."

The report around the circle blew me away. Member after member expressed clarity about the decision—a new ministry among homeless people in our own city, a cause equally thrilling to me. And every one of them wryly conveyed Jesus' solicitude for my bruised feelings.

Art indeed.

.   .   .   .   .   .

"Get Started"
· · · · · ·

I HAD JUST ARRIVED at a conference center in rural Virginia. Two cordial strangers collected me from the Richmond airport and they regaled me during the two-hour drive with hearty spiritual conversation tailored to paper over our foreignness to each other. Instead, however, the conversation heightened it. I'm an introvert, so under the circumstances you may imagine my nostrils flared slightly and my eyes glazed over.

The weeklong conference, for which I was one of two keynoters, was one of a number that year entitled "Camps Farthest Out," CFO for short, an ecumenical gathering of Charismatics with historical roots back into the 1920s.

CFO has a gallery of heroes whom the members delight telling about from year to year. My favorite anecdote concerns a fundamentalist/mystic named Rufus Mosely. Legend has it that he was once auditing a class in New Testament at the ultra-liberal Union Seminary in New York City. He was listening to a guest lecturer, a physician, somewhat superciliously disparaging any credibility for Jesus' virginal conception in medico-biological terms—something about Jesus coming out a haploid female. Rufus grew impatient and whispered to Jesus:

"Lord, are you there?"

"I'm right here, Rufus."

"Lord, were you really born of a virgin?"

"Sure was."

"That man up there doesn't believe that."

"That's right—but you have to love him anyway."

That may give you some sense of the prevailing spirituality at CFOs. Though as a liberal existentialist I normally feel somewhat out of place at their conferences, there's no denying their warmth and godliness. As someone said, they put the "fun" in Fundamentalism. I always wind up glad I went.

· · · · · ·

So I got moved in, had dinner, made a few acquaintances, and headed out afterwards for our first large meeting. My colleague, the other speaker, led off.

Before he spoke we had to have "worship." "Worship" comprised being led in a bunch of unappetizing songs by a woman who was introduced as a Baptist—the sort of Baptist the word "staunch" often attaches to. Dressed like a girls' school athletic director, she drove us through the rhythm, energetically punching the air with both fists. The songs furthermore seemed to have been selected by a medical student wannabe—they all had something to do with Jesus' Blood, as though his hematological functions were his only interesting feature. I was standing there trying to appear affable, but I was thinking, these people put the mental in Fundamentalism.

Uh, oh. There was the Presence right behind me, and again I knew better than to look back.

"Gray, next Saturday morning when you and that lady hug each other for the last time, you will love her so much you'll both be teary. Why don't you get started?"

"Uh, yessir. Good idea."

To my surprise, it wasn't difficult. Her love of God quickly became evident even in that dreadful music. She might have been singing about blood but she was loving a Person and his people, me included. Seeing her with new eyes, I spotted a potential buddy. So she proved. During the week we'd seek each other out at mealtimes, our discussions forming deeper and deeper "explorations into God." Daily she would attentively solicit my plans for the upcoming address so that her selections for preliminary songs and hymns might get the audience ready. Whereas I'd been braced against a potential adversary, I discovered a gracious discerning ally.

Somehow, the music got better without my having to correct her taste. Funny how that happens.

. . . . . .

AT THE TURN OF THE TWENTIETH CENTURY, a group of American Evangelicals, frightened and angered by the rising tide of scientific evidence that the Bible could no longer be taken as literal journalism, resolved to settle the matter by fiat. They set forth five "fundamentals" of the Christian faith, a shibboleth (cf. Judges 12) to separate the real Christians from the imposters. These included the inerrancy of the Old and New Testaments and, consequently, the insistence that the virginal conception of Jesus, his bodily Resurrection, and his Second Coming were (or in the latter instance would be) historical facts. The result was what we call Fundamentalism. You could, ironically, think of Fundamentalism as theological minimalism!

A lot of Charismatics buy all that uncritically. In fact that linkage is one of the chief reasons that thoughtful Episcopalians want little to do with the Charismatic Movement—or with "Charismatics."

But it's an accidental connection. There is nothing in the actual experience of being baptized in the Holy Spirit that requires it. Spirit-baptism may get you to love the Bible more than you did and recognize more of what it describes in your own experience. But if you were reading the Bible critically, making the same literary judgments you'd use in an airport selecting a paperback for a long flight ("This is poetry; that's prose—appears to be some sort of fiction. Aha—it's science fiction; believe I'll keep looking."), nothing about the Charismatic experience would require you to quit that and start buying it all literally.

So why the connection?

Most Episcopalians are not very receptive to having freshly Spirit-baptized people bursting into their parishes wanting to explain Christianity to everybody. The chilly reception they meet usually frustrates the new converts, so they migrate to other settings. A lot of people in those groups have the same experience in common: they've previously been sternly corrected and fussed at by mainline church leaders. Those leaders often appealed to extra-biblical authorities and traditions to make them hush, refusing to get pulled into discussions of what the Bible may or may not say. The new Charismatic never heard of Canon Law or the rubrics in the Book of Common Prayer or Richard Hooker's appeals to reason—you can't find that stuff in your motel room, so it's undemocratic to use it as a weapon, they conclude. They left their original denominations with a deep suspicion of the "traditions and doctrines of men." The Bible feels safer. And the Bible at least is public, not just the property of supercilious "experts." From now on, the Bible—and the Bible alone—would be their authority.

Interestingly, most Fundamentalists are not Charismatics. Fundamentalists usually believe that specific evidences of the Holy Spirit ceased with the close of the New Testament era, so they view Charismatic praying in tongues and reports of healings as spurious. But most Charismatics are, however, somewhat fundamentalist, because they relearned Christianity after their conversions among people for whom the Bible alone is authoritative.

When I arrived at St. Patrick's, I found that a number of erstwhile Episcopalians-gone-Charismatic had joined the parish, bringing lots of wounds, suspicions, and fundamentalist assumptions about the Bible with them. Many became my friends. Their love of God, their high delight in God's creation, and their courage in God's service could heat up an igloo.

One friend in particular was infectious with his genuine warmth. He and I eventually became prayer partners. Things worked fine as long as we simply prayed about stuff. Things got complicated when we began discussing them. When our disputes became as frequent as our prayers—and lasted longer— we quit meeting regularly. (Oddly, we remain friends even after many intervening years and vicissitudes.)

On one occasion when discussion preceded prayer, we quarreled. My friend described a trip he and his family had made to a science museum. They were looking at human fossils. The label on one said it dated from 10,000 B.C. Now, like many Fundamentalists, he subscribes to old Bishop Ussher's 4004 B.C. dating of Creation. So to his way of thinking 10,000 B.C.

was 5,996 years worth of mistake. Evidently he had loudly announced this obvious fact to his family, loudly enough, in fact, to edify everyone else in the hall.

I guess I winced at his pronouncement. I may have even ventured some regret at the silly impression he'd made on the other people, an impression that intelligent Christians would bear the brunt of. He jumped on my reaction, insisting I account for it. There's some chance my reply may not have been altogether flattering to his position (I recall mentioning the Flat Earth Society in scornful tones) because we were shortly going at each other hammer and tong.

Eventually our habit of friendship overrode our impulses to obliterate each other and we dropped the argument, agreeing to disagree. We spent some time in reparative prayer and went about our separate business.

But I was left pumping adrenaline, rueful that my "educated" position should be so painful to a friend I valued. I crept into the chapel and closed the door.

Kneeling at the altar, I poured out my misery to God. "God, you gave me my brain and you filled it with most of its present contents. I learned the scientific outlook at schools you sent me to. It's all your gift. If it's costing me friendships, you can have it back. My friend is a godly man and he swears I'm wrong. If I'm wrong, say so. Take it. If you want me to be a Fundamentalist, hell, I'll be a Fundamentalist."

"Are you finished?"

"Yessir."

"Are you willing for me to instruct, encourage, or correct you with any part of the Bible at all? Or are there sections you would rather I not use?"

"Lord, you can use the Atlanta phone book to guide me if you choose."

"That's exactly where I want you."

In retrospect, there are a lot of questions about the Bible I wish I'd asked while God was being talkative. But they didn't feel important at the time.

. . . . . .

I ONCE READ AN ARTICLE by an Atlanta neurologist stating that the first half hour of one's day sets the entire emotional tone for the rest. Years previously, a stuffy English bishop had offered my seminary classmates some dubious advice (though it suited us all well enough at the time): "Gentlemen, never confuse early morning metabolism with spirituality." Still when I read the neurologist's observation, it struck me as true. It also struck me as a prompt to begin taking my own prayer life more seriously. I decided to give God the first period of my day.

It became my habit to rise each morning at six and go to my chair in the study for Bible reading and prayer. The formats and lectionaries would vary, but the habit persisted. Sometimes it would be free prayer and Bible reading at random. In dry periods I would use the meditation procedure developed by St. Peter of Alcantara—a wise precursor of John of the Cross and Teresa of Avila.

I like this procedure a lot, especially when prayer feels burdensome. Similar to the later Ignatian methods, it requires you to imagine a biblical scene so vividly that it becomes an internal event for you, an element in your own story. Additionally, it requires you to take active ownership of Jesus' own virtues; it does so by asking you to offer Jesus' "merits" as *your* gift to the Father, implying that you have already signed the receipt. Furthermore, it instructs you to choose some especially trenchant moment from the meditation as a "spiritual nosegay," a flower to wear on your lapel all day and sniff at opportune moments.

However, my enthusiasm on any given morning could be as varied as my forms of prayer. Sleepiness was only one cause for dampened enthusiasm. If you're mad at somebody and have no intention of forgiving them, prayer proves challenging. In fact any insistence on self-justification—and who among us does not spend plenty of time in that tenuous position?—will find real prayer strenuous.

One morning I was in one of those states—I was up in my chair ready for prayer—but

I really did not want to talk to God. More to the point, I really didn't want God talking to me. Things were going on in my soul that I did not want God's comment on. Naturally I did not experience this state as active resistance to God—that would have been "bad" and I cannot comfortably think of myself as bad. In a semiconscious defense mechanism, I experienced my resistance to prayer as sleepiness. My head nodded downward and popped back up, threatening whiplash. Though I managed to keep my eyes open, I could hardly keep them uncrossed. Surely God couldn't be mad at me for being tired, tired-out in God's own service, come to think of it. Innocent.

Perhaps some music would help keep me awake. On my record changer I had a recording of the Chieftains, a traditional Irish band that plays animated stuff. Just the thing to stir the blood . . . and shut out the "still small Voice."

I hit the button and the room filled with Gaelic gaiety.

Suddenly I became aware of something right in front of me. A man's sandaled feet were visible beneath the hem of his robe. I did not look higher than his belted waist—because his feet were performing an intricate jig, with utter delight.

"Gray, your music will not keep me out of this room."

"Yessir."

■ ■ ■

I have reason to believe that's not the first time Jesus danced. On one such morning I was reading the story of the wedding at Cana in John 2. I read Greek pretty well and was struck that Jesus' reply to his mother, *"ti emoi kai soi?"* ("What to me and to you?" i.e., "What do we have to do with each other?") was the same phrase word for word as the Gadarene demons had shrieked at Jesus in Mark 5:7 just before their piggyback ride over the cliff into the lake. There was no getting around its abrasiveness.

"Lord, why were you so abrupt with your mother in this story?" I asked.

"She interrupted me when I was dancing."

VISUALIZING YOURSELF into a Bible scene can be a sweet exercise, wonderfully crafted for times when we don't feel like praying and need an agenda.

One morning, I was reading the episode in Luke 7:35ff about the prostitute who performs a pleasantness on our Lord's feet at a formal dinner. Imagining the scene vividly and sensuously, I found that I was more awake than was my wont at that hour. My pulse was racing. I wondered if Jean would mind being awakened.

I realized I was reading about an erotic act—right there in the gospel.

During the intellectual part of the meditation, in which you discuss the scene with Jesus himself, I began by expostulating, "Lord, that read like an erotic encounter!"

"It was indeed."

"Was that all right?"

"Gray, permit me to remind you whom you're addressing," he said gently.

"Er . . .excuse me . . . I guess it *must* have been okay; I mean, if it was you and all. . . ."

Then suddenly I found that I was spewing forth a lifetime of frustrated confusion—telling him how it felt to be raised a preacher's son in Calvinist eastern North Carolina (an implacable matriarchy masquerading as a patriarchy), horny years at an all-male boarding school with only occasional and heavily chaperoned glee club dances to relieve things, chaotically exhilarated yet scared all through college, all too diffident with Jean, immobilized nowadays around assertive or flirtatious women, on and on, telling Jesus about the inchoate anguishes of being a guy.

"Lord, when you were alive in the flesh, what did it feel like for *you* to be male? How did you handle that woman's attentions? How did *you* react to all the women around you? What did your *maleness* feel like to you?"

"Are you willing to be changed utterly by what I tell you?"

"Er . . . well . . . uh . . . what sort of change did you have in mind exactly. . . ?"

"When you can give me an unequivocal 'yes' to my question, then I'll answer your question."

Summoning the courage to offer that yes took the better part of the next decade—and only occurred in stages.

If you want to know what he answered, go ask him yourself.

A PSYCHOTHERAPIST HAD REFERRED a woman to me for a sacramental confession. He'd sounded worried. His client was suicidal and reported no particular belief in God. But unless she could reclaim membership in the human community, she would shortly take her leave of it. God is our ace in the hole. When you're reduced to being down to God, you're way down indeed. This woman was way down.

Our greeting as we first met was neither cordial nor energetic. The woman was sullen, depressed, and—as I was to learn—seized with a deep self-loathing. I explained the procedure for confession to her and led her to the chapel. She knelt at the altar rail, I sat in a chair just behind it. She began her confession.

My skin crawled.

While on active duty in the Air Force she had, for self-indulgent reasons, exercised her duty in a deliberately careless manner in order to precipitate an accident, knowing she'd be allowed off duty to visit her boyfriend while the accident was processed. In the event, the accident cost a couple of colleagues their lives. She knew that this tragedy was her own, deliberate fault. It would never have happened had she done her duty properly. Her erstwhile friends knew it, her superiors knew it. But for technical reasons she could not be touched. She had escaped the legal repercussions of her act. But all during the years since that night she had carried the contempt of her remaining colleagues along with her own. The burden was growing too heavy.

Governing my own revulsion, I pronounced formal absolution. On impulse I looked her in the eye. "Do you receive that?" I asked. What I saw in her responsive gaze was a cynical despair that made me drop my eyes.

"Of course not," she replied. "I'm not forgivable—and you know it."

I did know it. I agreed with her. If she had left the chapel and ended her own life at that

. . . .

moment, part of me would not have regretted her action.

In my spirit I cried out to Jesus, begging to know what hope there was for such a person.

In reply came a response that catalyzed the ultimate resolution.

"Ask her whom does she need to forgive."

"I wonder if anyone has ever hurt you real badly," I inquired.

"Yes, I guess so. I mean, not like *I* did, but it still hurts."

She then described the ragged ending of her marriage and her present messy estrangement from her former husband. He had left her in a lot of pain and cleaned her out financially in the bargain.

I suggested that it would be fruitful for her to work on forgiving him, and described to her the steps to forgiveness. We went through those steps slowly and in detail, taking our time. When you do it deliberately, you can really feel it. She felt it, weighed its cost. She did it anyway.

"I'm going to drop a pending court action against him," she promised.

"God. I'm a witness to that promise," I muttered.

"I'm going to quit speaking and thinking of him critically."

"God, I'm a witness to what she's promising."

"I'm going to quit using him as an excuse for my own nasty living since our divorce."

"God I'm a witness to what she's committing."

And on and on.

At the end she was sweating. I was too.

"Have you managed to forgive him, to make him a gift of all the trouble he gave you?" I asked.

"Yes, I think I really have," she replied.

"Good—then let's try your own confession again."

We went back through her confession.

"Bless me, for I have sinned."

She repeated the whole terrible story. This time I stood, put my hand on her head, signed her forehead with the Cross, and in Jesus' name pronounced her forgiven.

"Do you receive *that*?" I asked, once more looking her in the eye, this time without dropping my gaze. She couldn't speak. She simply nodded—and neither of us spoke again for a long time.

She was back safe inside the human community.

IN SPITE OF BEING A MERRY PLACE, St. Patrick's remained a tumultuous community for the first five years I was there. The old member/new member conflict took a long while to dissipate, predictable issues like the introduction of folk masses and guitars providing ever-present fodder. At lunch one day, the bishop spotted my fatigue and low-level depression and suggested a sabbatical. The vestry agreed.

English friends offered us a cottage in a village outside Oxford. A letter to Walter Hooper, C.S. Lewis's amanuensis and literary executor, secured an offer of direction for a course of reading at the Bodleian Library at Oxford University, and St. Patrick's parishioners pooled their frequent flier miles to get us there—and back. Jean's sister, her brother-in-law, a comptroller for American Express on assignment outside London, and our nieces were living on an ancient estate; a sabbatical over there would give us a chance to visit them. All in all, it looked providential.

We ended up spending the first two weeks with the in-laws because our cottage near Oxford wasn't quite ready. They were generous with their car. It was right-hand drive, so they were brave to lend it.

My depression grew pronounced in that unaccustomed setting. The food tasted weird and the beer didn't taste like it had in Germany. The plumbing was temperamental. They had a swimming pool, but even in June only a polar bear would use it. Though southern England was exotic to us, nothing about Americans was exotic over there. The people we dealt with were matter-of-fact and curt, evincing no interest or wish to get to know us. Even as an introvert, I shortly found myself lonesome.

We went to the village market one day, simply to be part of a crowd. As I wandered among the stalls, I was drawn toward a man selling shoes, boots and laces. He was a burly giant, his large florid head thatched with wild yellow hair and beard. Desperate for more

. . . . . .

than a few short words, I bought a pair of shoelaces and deliberately paid with a £20 note, requiring lots of change and likely a comment.

Sure enough. Making change, he looked at me quizzically and asked, "A Yank, are ye?"

That seemed no time to quibble. I allowed as much.

"I've been to Florida, I have," he ventured.

Not a very promising opening gambit, I supposed, but gambit it was.

"Oh?" I replied, "And what did you do there?"

"Went to Disney World, I did,"

Great, just great.

"And I went to the Billy Graham Crusade!"

Aha! A Christian believer, drawing his ICHTHYS fish in the dust!

"Are you a Christian?" I asked.

Indeed he was. He, a Scotsman, was in fact an elder in his local conventicle, entrusted with oversight for their healing ministries. I asked about his exercise of it.

"Let me show ye," he offered, reaching out both hands. My hands disappeared between his. He lifted up his face towards heaven—and the lights went on. A warm smile of utter trust took over his whole form. He prayed:

"Ooooooh, Father! Congratulations for my brother here!" On and on he went. My body was filled with a sense of safety, a sense of belonging right there. It was timeless, transcendent.

I think I got healed on the spot of ailments I didn't know I had.

For what it's worth, the Scotsman's ministry has formed the basis of my own understanding of healing ministry ever since. Likely there are people who are able, by the laying on of hands, to convey some actual healing force into the bodies of those they touch—in India they call this force *prana*. But for the rest of us there is another way: we simply hold onto the suffering person and begin to trust and love God in the setting of our common distress.

God takes it from there.

. . . . . .

AFTER A COUPLE OF WEEKS, our cottage was ready. Jean's sister generously loaded up their spacious (for England) car and we set off northwest. The cottage was fairly modern in a dignified way, matching the neighborhood. Thatch-roofed pubs were within walking distance, as was a bakery and a small grocer's. Our back garden adjoined an old abbey church. Dating from the eleventh century, it marked the spot where in 634 St. Birinus had baptized King Cynygyls of the West Saxons. We could still see the creek.

Late the first night we were awakened by my older son, screaming with stomach pains. Because Charles is normally quite healthy and uncomplaining, we knew something was seriously wrong. Appendicitis seemed the friendliest, most likely explanation. In the borrowed car, with Jean holding Charles in the back seat, I raced off toward Oxford. The whole time I was desperately trying to remember how to make right and left turns from the left lane. Thank God it was late at night and there was virtually no traffic.

The tourists' Oxford is a small picturesque section of the city. The actual metropolitan area is vast and modern. I was clueless—the welter of cries and whimpers from the backseat, the puzzling European street signs, and the disorientation of driving into what felt like oncoming traffic all had me verging on panic.

Suddenly a flashing light in my rearview mirror caught my attention—a car signaled me to stop. Not a cop—no blue lights on the roof. I pulled over, managing to recall it must be to the left curb. A leather-clad man leaned into my window.

"You're a Yank, right?"

["This is not a good time for a lesson in regional humility, Lord!"]

["Put up with it."]

"And you're lost, seems like."

"How did you know?" I asked, pointlessly.

· · · · · ·

"You're driving wildly and you ran up a one-way street just now. Follow me."

"Follow you? Follow you *where*?"

"Why, to the Radcliffe Infirmary—that's the best hospital in these parts."

As he pulled ahead, I saw he was a cab driver. He led us on a merry chase through many city blocks, the streets mercifully empty. I didn't have time to wonder how he'd known we sought a hospital. Finally he pulled over beside a large building and pointed to the door. He sped away before I could thank him. I recalled having seen a gold cross around his neck.

Charles proved to be okay—a severe case of gastritis, gently and easily treated by lovely nurses and physicians. Getting home an hour or so after arriving was a lot simpler than the trip in had been.

■ ■ ■

The next Sunday we attended the main service at the abbey church over the back wall. Since we were late, we ended up sitting in front.

I studied the lovely surroundings, some nearly a thousand years old. The altar rail in front of me looked new—a discordant aesthetic touch, I thought. The inscription drew my eye: it had recently been given to the church in memory of a man I knew, Malcolm Strachan, the chaplain at Groton School in New England where I'd spent my boyhood.

I wondered if we might not have been brought to the right place.

OUR LIFE IN ENGLAND that summer was largely pleasant. I got used to being called a "Yank," or (worse) a "colonial." And for that snobbish reason I still prefer Germany and France to England—since I retain a fair amount of German from college and French from Groton. On the Continent my speech marks me as one who has gone to a whole lot of trouble to bridge the gap between countries and cultures—not as someone to be patronized. At least one pleasant upper-class lady remarked to me, "I can tell by your speech that you're American—yet your accent is neither harsh nor unpleasant!" I was able to tell her that in my dulcet Southern tones she doubtless recognized the ancestor of her own "Received Pronunciation" ("the Queen's English"), which only dates from the early nineteenth century.

Our next-door neighbors, Colin and Brian, the first gay couple Jean and I had ever socialized with, greeted us warmly. A long-cherished stereotype of gay effeminacy bit the dust as we learned that Brian had been a pilot in the Strategic Air Service—a select group of hardened commandos with whom one does not lightly mess. Colin and Brian arranged for a friend to lend me a motorbike for the whole summer, allowing me to putt in and out of Oxford at will. Jean climbed on back for evening pub visits. Once when she took our boys to visit their long-separated relatives in Scotland, Colin and Brian led me on a merry pub crawl, ending up at their house where they taught me to value Richard Strauss—a gift for which I remain grateful.

The local rector and his wife, Ray and Barbara, became our friends. (The idea of a sabbatical fascinated him—he later took a sabbatical of his own with us at St. Patrick's in Atlanta.) I described to Ray the depression and discouragement which had led to my summer away from home. He wondered if I thought simply reading all day—even in the splen-

. . . . . .

dor of the Duke Humphrey Reading Room—would sufficiently exorcise the demons I continued to battle. He graciously offered me a key to the abbey church and suggested that on weekdays its lovely emptiness would be an ideal setting for personal reflection—"where prayer has been valid."

I leapt at his offer and quickly fell into a pattern of spending each Tuesday there for most of the day. I would fast, do devotional readings, work in my journal, and attempt to sense Jesus' Presence in prayer.

It took most of the summer.

One August day as I was fasting in St. Birinus' Chapel, I finally had a sense that I was no longer alone. Without taking visible form (other than all the medieval windows, the statuary, and the Reserved Sacrament) Jesus stood/sat/hovered/*was* in front of me.

It was time for a direct conversation. All summer long I had struggled with a sense of failure in my profession. I had ruminated long and hard about alternative vocations. Now I could ask God directly and anticipate a direct answer.

"What do you want me to do?"

"I want you to return to St. Patrick's."

"For how long?"

"For the rest of your life, if I so decide."

"It'll kill me!"

"It won't kill you if you tell the truth."

That reply annoyed me. In the South where I grew up, untruths used to be considered dishonorable; Groton hadn't favored them either. I would scorn myself for lying under any circumstances I could conceive.

I bristled.

"I'm not aware of lying to those people, Lord."

"Consider how often you have pretended to know what you were doing when you did not. Think

of how often you were angry or frightened and made as though all were well."

"Oh—you mean *that*?"

"Yes—I mean that. *If you return and resolve to be truthful, you will find it suits you well."*

That broke my depression. A new sense of challenge replaced the previous discouragement. I recalled the conversation of a couple of years previous in which I was seated on the hearth, witnessing the vision of a mature people. Now I knew what sort of leadership was necessary to permit such a community to evolve.

. . . . . .

MY FAMILY AND I returned from England in the fall of 1979 to a surprisingly calm parish. I had missed them, I discovered. And they had actually missed me. Not a bad place to spend my life, I mused.

You can't tell if you're being obedient to God unless you get tested. I almost flunked my first test. As so often happens, God took my near-failure and transformed it into an experience I'd hate to have missed.

The test of whether I was to remain at St. Patrick's came in the form of an invitation to interview for a position as dean of a seminary. My prospects seemed at least fair because various people involved in the decision favored my candidacy.

As these things do, the process dragged on for months. I kept the matter close to my chest—no sense in disrupting a parish that was enjoying relative calm. So all during this period I put a moratorium on Jesus' instruction to tell the truth. That's a pretty strenuous way to live, especially among people you love. By the time the news arrived, I was tired of dragging the suspense around.

The phone call came during a counseling session with a distraught parishioner. I left the room to get on another phone, was told by the embarrassed caller that the committee had selected a former professor of mine for the position. I stiffened my upper lip, congratulated him on the committee's splendid choice, squared my shoulders, and rejoined my tearful sheep, who required undistracted attention that I was at pains to offer.

In the Episcopal Church, we call competitions for positions "races." That's only partially accurate. In a foot race, everyone crosses the finish line, though only one breaks the tape. In our professional races, there is no finish line—there is an opening in a wall through which only one can fit. The rest of the runners slam full force into the wall.

So it was with me. I was frozen, and knew that when I could feel again the sensation

· · · · · ·

would not be pleasant. So I betook myself to the office of a psychotherapist friend who knew all about the process I'd been through. I told him I'd lost. He asked how I felt about it. I didn't know. So he began to probe and delve here and there.

Towards the end of the hour I was starting to get in touch with my feelings—as they say—and they were lousy.

"I think I know how I feel," I ventured.

"I think I can guess," he responded.

"Yeah, I think I'm going to get depressed."

"I think you are too."

"What should I do about it?" I asked.

"Nothing," he replied.

"*Nothing?*"

"Nothing."

"I'm supposed to be the one in here that's crazy. But you're not making any sense," I protested.

"Let me explain. Your depression is the result of an energy shift. The depression itself is energy and will get you deeper into your unconscious than you can normally go. It is message laden. Ride this depression like a horse—see where it takes you."

I dragged through the next couple of days as one recently bereaved, circumstance after circumstance abruptly reminding me of what felt like a loss. Finally I felt driven to apply my friend's instruction.

The next day I drove to Charlotte, North Carolina, to keynote a conference in a friend's parish. When I arrived at Bill's home, I found out that my afternoon was free. I immediately asked him if I might use his guest room for a badly needed nap.

Safely sequestered in the guest room with uninterrupted hours in front of me, I rolled up my sleeves. I prayed briefly for help and direction. Then I addressed the depression face on, telling it to take its best shot. "If you can kill me, go ahead and try."

This time Jesus didn't speak. He gave me a vision instead. I saw my depression as a darkness-piercing searchlight, one of those huge World War II anti-aircraft lights rented nowadays by car dealers, aimed directly at me. The pain of looking at it corresponded to the grief I'd been feeling—and evading—about being passed over. I turned my back to the beam's source and looked down along its path. The darkness it pierced was my own inner life, dark because long unexamined. Things that I had not faced up to for a long period got clear in that light's judgment, and as each thing got judged, it ceased either to pain or embarrass me. For example, the vanity I had invested in the new position got fully exposed, and suddenly looked not shameful but comic. I had been thinking anything I wrote would get published just by dint of my position. That laziness fell away from me, exposed as dishonorable. The anticipation of an unearned doctorate went with it, its tail between its legs.

As my metaphorical eyes grew accustomed to that light and trusted its revealing and healing impact, I was able to turn back and look at its source. Jesus himself was standing behind it; his hands gripped the handles on either side of it, directing the light, smiling mischievously with affectionate delight.

It took several rounds of about fifteen minutes apiece, punctuated by frequent catnaps to recover strength and courage. At length it was over. I was left empty, cleansed, calm, and merrily relieved to remain at St. Patrick's, doing what I was doing.

I had the physical shakes for the next day or so simply from the effort. But the depression itself was broken.

. . . . . .

AFTER HAVING JESUS penetrate your space from time to time with personal instructions or messages, you get where you sometimes sense, all of a sudden, that conversations with other people become Jesus himself talking to you. A lot of people I know are more sensitive to this effect than I am. When one finally gets through to me, it's almost like a gong going off right beside me. The gong's message says, *"Pay attention!"* I think this is the sort of thing that Charismatic buddies describe as "prophetic."

One of the first times I ever sensed Jesus alerting me to pay attention to what someone else was saying to me occurred as I made my first confession in front of Jim Radebaugh. I laid out a series of vanities that I confessed as the sin of pride. Expecting to be fussed at, I was surprised by Jim's gentle voice, sounding for all the world like another:

"Gray, a good trick to managing vanity is simply to become grateful for what you've been proud of. That way you get to keep the pleasure but avoid sin's poison."

■■■

There was a woman at St. Patrick's, a long-time parishioner, whose conversations were just about like talking directly to Jesus. Jane was a flamboyant redhead, a former torch singer, and a recovering alcoholic who probably sponsored half the AA members in the city, and a woman unhesitantly and passionately in love with Jesus Christ. That made even her casual utterances dangerous, since as likely as not they arose from her constant contact with him. You could strike a match on her eyeball without her blinking.

Jane was also a painter. One summer, wanting the children of St. Patrick's to know God's friendliness, she ordered everyone to stay out of the Sunday school wing for a couple of weeks. When she let us back in, the walls were covered with winsome murals based on Bible scenes. One particularly delightful mural shows our Lord, beaming with pleasure, seated with children of all ages, sexes, and races crawling into his lap. One of the children holds a chocolate ice cream cone that is dripping onto Jesus' white robe. Jane had also painted a merry sign in the nursery: "We Shall Not All Sleep—But We Shall All Be Changed."

■ ■ ■

A year or so after arriving at St. Patrick's, Jean and I offered a retreat for married couples, taking twelve couples to a mountain retreat center. We began by asking everyone to list on paper all the things about their partners they'd like to see changed—planning to ask the people to tear up the lists as a preliminary to a weekend of self-examination. But we were comically derailed. The husbands all hesitated, wrote some stuff, stared at it, erased it, hesitated, and wrote something else. In contrast, the wives all urgently requested more paper and more time. The contrast of hope with experience, we concluded.

During a group discussion, Jane began an observation: "When God wants to teach us something, God puts us in a situation where we can learn it. If we flee the situation, God puts us in another one until. . . ."

". . . Until we learn the lesson," I concluded for her, confident that I knew what she was talking about.

"No, Gray—until we learn to *love* that lesson."

BONG!

Before I could catch the words, I heard myself breathing, "Then, God, please teach me to love conflict!"

In seminary they don't teach you how to fight. Instead they tell you heroic stories of (a very few) distinguished graduates who manage their congregations either by warm pastoral cajoling or by cowing them with august charismatic personal authority and integrity. Neither style works very well when *you* try them, as most of us soon discovered.

So Jane's words became a prophecy.

■ ■ ■

God has been faithful to Jane's prophecy. I think I can honestly report that for the last few years I've enjoyed everything about conflict except the anticipation of it. (If God allowed me to enjoy the anticipation, I'd get dangerous.)

Most of our social behavior is aimed at anxiety reduction. Other people make us nervous, so we shade the truth, act over-cordial, make promises that prove difficult to keep, parade hunches as facts. For genuine intimacy to develop, we have to get past that with people, a process that is sometimes explosive. In conflict we learn truth, we develop trust, we cultivate self-restraint and self-soothing.

The red type in your New Testament marks sayings that mostly occurred in some fight or other, most of which Jesus himself provoked.

I think Jesus was speaking to me through Jane that day.

MY FRIEND, LARRY, collected me at the puddle-jumper in Rapid City, South Dakota near the Wyoming line. I was conducting a retreat for the men of the Diocese of Wyoming, an event he directed. We drove west along a flat highway.

Far over on the right, shortly after we crossed into his state, I saw a landmark I recognized both from a previous trip and from the film *Close Encounters Of The Third Kind*—Devil's Tower, the core of an eroded volcano, rising a thousand feet into the empty sky like a gigantic tree stump.

"Lots of guys climb that," my friend remarked.

"Hmmm—sounds like fun," I lazily remarked, assuming there were hiking trails to the top.

"You interested?" he said.

"Well, sure," I replied, "I don't get out here much."

"I'll see if I can arrange it for Monday," he said, ending a conversation to which I had paid insufficient attention.

At the conference he introduced me to Alex, whom he explained would be my guide on Monday. Alex looked at me quizzically, opened his mouth as if to ask me something, changed his mind, shook his head and walked off.

Throughout the weekend, I noticed a number of men at the retreat looked at me oddly. I didn't understand why; I didn't think I looked all that different from them. A couple of them asked me, "You climb a lot back East?"

"You mean with ropes and stuff? Heck no!" I'd reply.

They'd just stare.

I grew suspicious.

Before we parted Sunday after lunch Alex explained Monday's plan with me. A friend of his who is close to my size would lend me the special tight shoes climbers wear, as well as a chalk bag for palm friction. I was to take off my wedding ring, so my hands won't get stuck in a crack. I'd carry a spare rope. I wouldn't carry extra carabineers or chocks; Alex would be carrying them for the three of us (a third climber, Ed, had been enlisted), but I'd need to carry a pack with lots of water.

Jesus! We were going to *climb* the damn thing, not just *walk* up!

I struggled not to show panic. Too many people knew I was to make the climb for me to be able to back out now with any dignity.

When I was next alone I prayed—earnestly. "Lord, this is terrible. I've got myself in a mess. I can't climb a mountain straight up! I'll get killed."

"Gray, on Monday I'm going to climb Devil's Tower with those two guys. I'd enjoy having your company."

The borrowed shoes fit like tightened clamps. The chalk bag on my belt felt like it held a grapefruit; it swung, making balance tricky. I complained that the safety harness around my groin was somewhat tight, but my companions grinned and remarked that a little pinching would prove a worthwhile trade-off. They were right.

Climbers take it in stages—called "pitches." The leader gets to a stopping point, usually a small ledge, offering traction as he controls the safety rope belaying those below him. On an established route like the one we selected, experts have already cemented permanent pitons into the rock at various points into which hinged aluminum loops called carabineers can be clipped. The climbers can jam aluminum hexagons, perforated with loops of steel cable, called chocks, into cracks for additional stability. These get jerked free as the climbers pass them.

Most of the route lay in "chimneys"—narrow crevices in the rock face that enclosed us like a narrow alley between skyscrapers.

I was second on the rope, the safest position. Alex went first, free-climbing to the top of the first pitch, over one hundred feet above us, placing chocks in various crevices and clipping his safety rope to their loops with carabineers. Ed and I belayed him from below. Had Alex fallen—and had his chocks held—he would have pendulumed twice the distance below him from his highest chock. He didn't fall.

I followed the exact route Alex had chosen, tracing the safety rope up past his chocks. Ed came up third, free-climbing whatever route he chose since I'd removed each chock as I passed it. Since Ed was belayed from above, he would be safe no matter where he fell. He didn't fall.

I, on the other hand, did fall—a lot. Alex was above me, secured at the top of the pitch, belaying me with a turn of rope around his abdomen.

"Falling!" I would yell, trying not to actually shriek.

"Gotcha," Alex would call, and I would indeed fall no further than a foot or so, swing against the abrasive rock face until I could regain purchase, govern my breathing and pulse, and once more yell, "Climbing."

I wanted to cry, especially anytime I looked down, which I learned to quit doing. I wanted my daddy. I'd been told to keep three points of contact with the rock at all times—I had no trouble remembering that. Hell, I'd have used my *teeth* if I could have. I wished I had a prehensile navel.

"Falling," I yelled for the fourth time on that first pitch.

Then a voice came from above me. I knew it was Alex, but it sounded for all the world like another:

"Man, the only trouble with falling is that you eventually have to climb back past where you fell from."

There went that BONG again.

I recalled Jesus' invitation to make this climb with him. It occurred to me that nothing was happening that was not intended. I began praying my way up the chimney. "Holy Spirit, where is the next hand hold?" "Can I lean back right against the other wall now?" "Where does my foot go?"

I did not fall again that day.

It took seven hours and all our water to reach the grassy top—from which it seemed we could see half the world. A screw-top industrial pipe held a notebook and pencil where we inscribed our names, the date, and our comments. The rangers keep them on file. (One day I'm going to show my grandchildren that notebook.)

It took less than an hour to descend in several exhilarating rappels. That's what the rope I'd carried was for. We were splotched with sweat-glued dust, the backs of our hands and knuckles were raw from jamming our fists into cracks, and we were grinning like three mules eating briars.

A tour bus full of Germans stopped near us as we approached our truck.

"That looks very difficult," remarked one lady with a thick middle-European accent.

Recalling my college German, I replied, "Oh no, Madame—it's an agreeable climb if you know what you're doing. But you do have to be in training."

IN 1981 I went around the world.

I was a delegate from the Episcopal Church to an international gathering of members of Sharing of Ministries Abroad (SOMA), an organization that links Charismatic Anglicans from industrial and developing nations. After a week or so in Singapore, where the gathering was to be held, I would team up with another priest, Philip, and conduct teaching missions and consultations in dioceses across Southern Asia.

In those days Pan-American Airlines offered a ticket advertised as "Around the World in 80 Days." For $1,200 you could travel for six weeks in one direction, making at least four seventy-two hour stops. You rode First Class . . . on stand-by.

This journey was my first pilgrimage, that is, it was the first journey I had ever made with a manifestly spiritual purpose—to offer God a chance to engage me in new ways that would leave me changed. In describing it now, I'll have to peel off lots of exotic details—the constant novelty and the occasional risk—and simply try to lay out the context for conspicuous occasions when it seemed that Jesus entered my space in ways that made a redemptive difference.

Even before it began, the trip had a spooky feel. I had great difficulty getting out of town; at times I felt as if I were slashing my way through thick underbrush. Friends who know more about this kind of thing than I am ever likely to learn tell me such a struggle is typical whenever we embark on a significant spiritual event. You get the feeling that hell opposes it.

One sure sign for me that hell is trying to pollute a significant upcoming event is that Jean and I always have heated disagreements ahead of time—quarreling about all sorts of matters we normally let slide. The fight before this trip was a doozy. We were at each other constantly for a couple of weeks prior to my departure. I realized I had to pray about what was going on.

"You are reluctant to be separated for such a long time and are grieving before the separation even takes place. Learn to appreciate what is happening right now."

I reported that to Jean. She instantly agreed with its truth and we argued no further.

The pilgrimage was starting before it started.

The first leg of my trip was to New York with a stop in Washington. I'd arranged to overnight in New York with an old boarding school chum and board a flight for Tokyo the next morning.

So much for the best-laid plans. The February sky darkened as we took off from Washington. My seatmate was a charming Arab-Catholic woman married to a diplomat and fortunately we found ourselves to be very congenial. I say fortunately because after two character-building attempts to land in New York through impenetrable snow, we were returned to Washington for the night. Her husband and son graciously seconded her invitation to spend the night at their home before we set off again in the morning.

At National Airport the next day, I had the first of several trials: since I had a standby ticket, and since so many flights had been delayed or cancelled, I was unlikely to be able to board a flight for New York anytime soon. I was walking down one of those corridors at National, fretting about the delay, when I sensed the Presence:

"Gray, I can get you on that flight one of two ways: one with you worrying, the other with you not worrying. Which would you prefer?"

I opted for the second, which turned out to be a good choice; I made the flight. We had similar discussions repeatedly, he and I, all around the world in the coming days.

. . . . . .

A Pilgrim out of Place?

· · · · · ·

THE NEXT TWO LEGS of the flight took me from New York to Tokyo and from Tokyo to Hong Kong. Each flight was overbooked, each offered a renewed conversation about worry. But the deal held in spite of my constant fretting. I got seats on both flights, smooth as a Virginia reel.

I spent a week in Hong Kong recovering from jet lag. My hosts, Connie and Steve, were the sister and brother-in-law of my closest friend, Doug, a man I'd last seen back home, where he was dying of cancer. That first night, we got a phone call from his mother: Doug had died forty-five minutes after I arrived at their flat. I was the only man in Asia who had known Doug personally and I think we were all grateful that I was with them when they received word of his death. The week gave us time to grieve together.

Connie and Steve were missionaries. It was my first contact with missionaries in their adopted homes. I soon discovered that either being a missionary or visiting one is not for the faint-hearted. Steve and Connie themselves were charming friends, but as the week progressed and we discussed their work, a grim picture of life on the mission field emerged. Their station's mission team was torn by mutual disloyalties and suspicions, all of it internal. The missionaries from England, Scotland, and America seemed to me to illustrate Mark Twain's wisecrack about "great nations divided by a common language." That sort of discord was to become familiar on each mission station I visited. At the time I did not suspect that addressing those pains would be a primary focus of my visits to different mission compounds across Asia.

The SOMA conference in Singapore turned out to be as mixed an experience as showering in a cheap motel: searing heat battling chilling cold, never, for a moment, blending into uniform warmth.

Among the more positive experiences, I met and re-met wonderful friends. In James Mundia, a bishop from western Kenya, I recognized a young priest Jean and I had hosted in seminary years before. His teaching and preaching, as well as that of his fellow Africans, black and white, was, for me, the high point of the conference both spiritually and conceptually. The most unsettling element of the conference came from the West, from the United States and the United Kingdom. The differences were striking.

Whereas African-led worship was wonderfully energetic and spirited, Western-led worship was strident.

The Africans were clear about their real enemies: the devil, disease, ignorance, oppression, and poverty. The Western delegates for the most part were equally clear about their enemies: their bishops and colleagues back home who would not punch their tickets.

To my ears at least, the Asian and African teachings sounded fresh, constructed for the needs of this gathering, in this spot, on this occasion. The Western teachings were taken from each teacher's "Best of . . . " series, teachings that might have been fresh and (more to the point) impressive years ago and somewhere else, but which here sounded peevish.

All Western references to theology or biblical scholarship were uniformly contemptuous, as though the only motive for such work were supercilious impiety.

("Lord, have any of these clowns read any real biblical scholarship—say, Raymond Brown or somebody in his class?"

"Shhhhh. Besides, the only clown in this gathering is myself.")

All of the Africans and most of the Westerners were what we'd call "Fundamentalists." But for the Africans, that meant simply trusting the Bible to point directly to Jesus, the real focus of interest. The Westerners' variety of Fundamentalism was a bibliolatry that never pointed anywhere close to Jesus, but often to criticisms of others' motives and/or sexuality. To be this sort of Fundamentalist and to be a functional atheist at the same time is not so wide a stretch as it may sound. That is to say, one has little awareness among such people of the presence of Jesus Christ as a personal figure, for all their preoccupation with earnest religious abstractions.

· · · · · ·

A prominent English evangelist at one point delivered an acerbic prophecy in front of the group, loudly proclaiming God's condemnation on bishops and church leaders in the United Kingdom who would not embrace "renewal," joyously anticipating their personal destruction. You may not have ever heard someone doing that. This one started out with, "Thus says the Lord, the Almighty: *Woe* to you bishops, you false lying false shepherds. . . ."

As he ranted, I found myself whispering, "Lord, is that *you* talking?" The answer was a tactful silence, one that left me internally jammed-up.

At a break I approached the evangelist and said to him, "I tried to pray as you were delivering that message to us; it seemed to be more your own stuff than Jesus'. How about praying about what you were saying to see if it was all really from God."

He replied without hesitation, "And, Brother, I urge *you* to pray to see what it is in *you* that cannot accept such a word!"

A cloud already hovering above me lowered. I sank toward depression. At a worship service that evening I was in despair, wondering what I was doing here in such a gathering. My old friend James preached. His text was 2 Corinthians 12:9b, "My grace is sufficient for you, for [my] power is made perfect in weakness." I barely heard it. All I could do was ask God what was I doing here. I felt like an imposter. If these were the sort of people that God wanted traveling all over the world to teach the Church, did I belong among them? My despair approached panic.

Then the import of James' words reached me and I felt the Presence. I took my own advice to the bellicose English evangelist and prayed. "I sure hope your strength *is* made perfect in weakness, Lord. I sure am weak at this moment."

"Gray, you ask what you're doing here. At the moment what you are doing is making a place for your enemy."

I recognized that in deciding to despise my Western colleagues, I'd allowed the despair and panic to coalesce into a spiritual assault, an onslaught that would immobilize me and keep me from doing whatever I was supposed to do at this conference and beyond it. I had tricked myself into believing it was up to me to marshal some sort of personal ability, wisdom, or skill in the ministries that lay before me. Heartened at hearing Jesus' voice again, I relaxed and enjoyed being weak, enjoyed not knowing what I was doing. I quit worrying about whether or not I belonged in this gathering—I was just there. I quit worrying about sounding wise or spiritual—I just said whatever seemed to make sense at the moment. I quit worrying about sounding like a beginner and asked questions of people who appeared to know what they were talking about.

The result was that the gathering began to feel comfortable. I was aware of a sense of kinship with the others. An Englishwoman who gave an impassioned lecture to us about the importance of women seeking a lower place than men (Why? Why to *this* gathering? Jeez!) became a buddy I could tease. (Not that she ever laughed, mind you.) The *pièce de résistance* came the final night during the concluding service: the English evangelist sought me out for a long un-English hug. Maybe he'd forgotten who I was.

In any event, it felt like a benediction.

Burma

. . . . . .

IN THE EARLY '80s, a Westerner could still get into Burma for a week's visit, but the government was largely Marxist and deeply anti-Western. Only the Buddhist element in their culture encouraged any tolerance at all for the indigenous churches. Missionaries from outside were anathema. So if you were a priest from the outside, you had to tell them you were a teacher, otherwise the government would not allow you to address a religious meeting.

Rangoon was the most "foreign" place I'd ever been. The architecture was a mixture of British colonial and Buddhist. It was tropical and utterly lovely. The people were poor, but uniformly so—I was grateful to be spared the drastic contrasts between wealth and abject poverty one sees in America's economic colonies. The men and women all wore the sarongs we learned to call *longhis*. The women knotted theirs to the side, the men knotting theirs at the front in a vaguely phallic arrangement.

I had a *longhi* made for myself, combining two, truth be known, given a certain difference in my stature from that of the average Burmese. Naively I wore the thing downstairs into the lobby of my hotel. "When in Rome. . . ." You know how it is. I ignored a couple of pesky locals on the down elevator, nor had I felt the slight tug at my artless, neophyte knot.

As I passed the ladies at the front desk my *longhi* fell about my ankles. I bent over red-faced and tried desperately to haul it back up, in the process getting it hopelessly entangled in the camera that hung low from my neck. The women working the reception desk laughed merrily every time they saw me for the rest of the week.

I particularly remember—and miss—the smells of Rangoon. I've wondered since then if we in the West ever really use our noses. Close your eyes and try to imagine a combination of fragrances and odors: tropical flowers, fish, and kerosene, all wafting through the air on an underlying base of charcoal smoke. That smell was there all the time, everywhere, eventually permeating your hair, your clothing, and your very pores.

. . . . . .

The people on the street were polite and deeply helpful—merrily friendly. I met a black marketeer on the street the first afternoon and brushed him off, displaying my Atlanta police chaplain's I.D. which names me a captain. I subsequently saw him repeatedly at church meetings; it turned out he was a church leader. We always winked at each other.

My partner Phil and I were to speak, teach, and consult all over the city of Rangoon; the archbishop determined our schedule each day. James' Singapore teaching from the SOMA conference was never far from my mind: I was keenly aware of my own weakness, not knowing the culture or the people or their local needs. Yet our time was most fruitful. Again and again the need arose to name to the missionaries patterns of local distrust and resentment we were discerning.

In addition to all the stresses any church anywhere experiences, churches in Burma had to contend with rivalries between different tribes (Burma has seven major groups) and various immigrant nationalities.

And again and again they seemed to hear us.

Phil and I got to address a clergy conference and a class of theological students. As I said, tribalism is deeply rooted in Burma, a country whose ethnic groups form rival powerblocks. That situation is intensified by post-colonial leftover populations of Tamils, other Indians, and Chinese, each viewing themselves as superior to everybody and resented by all. We discussed the spiritual and social dangers of tribalism, demonstrating from Ephesians and Colossians that some New Testament writers thought overcoming tribalism was the core of the very gospel itself. Some seemed to hear the message and to consider repentance.

And we addressed issues other than tribalistic rivalries. Some members of the clergy asked for help to heal their marriages; others confronted patterns of sexual molestation of parishioners; we prayed with alcoholic clergy and planted the germ of Alcoholics Anonymous with two of them.

Several days into the trip Phil and I felt like taking a break. We went walking across the city, intent on seeing the zoo. On our way, Phil was regaling me animatedly (probably scolding me for favoring women's ordination) when, with a cry, he dropped out of sight, into an open concrete sewage ditch neither of us had seen. I grabbed him under the shoulders and lifted him out in one of those adrenal spurts of strength chronicled in so many *Readers' Digest* stories. He was moaning in agony, his shin was torn and bloody with a dangerously septic scrape.

I have never felt so far from home, so far from anything or anybody *safe*.

Then from over my shoulder came the sense of being on familiar ground:

"I am here."

"Then help!" I cried inside as I began to pray aloud for Phil's comfort.

"Perhaps you would allow me to be of assistance?" came a gently refined Asian voice. A Burmese gentleman who spoke perfect English stood there offering his services. He summoned a taxi, relayed our hotel address to the cabby, and off we sped.

Back in the room I bathed Phil's shin with purified water (I carried a katadyne filter) and a bottle of Betadine. Our combined first-aid kits contained enough bandages to make a patch.

Phil napped, recovered his equanimity, and offered a splendid teaching that night at the service.

All during that week, I was aware of Jesus being easy to contact, in front of me with instructions and often with needed courage. It was simply important for me to stay empty enough for him to fill the gaps. Learning to think of oneself as without resources, as inadequate for one's tasks, feels counter-intuitive. I was learning in a powerful way that cultivating that posture as a spiritual discipline makes room for God to happen.

■ ■ ■

One afternoon I was in the archbishop's garden, struck with the beauty of the tropical flowering trees. A sadness struck me as I realized that I would never see the archbishop, or his family again in this life, or his canon, Peter, who'd I'd begun a friendship with in Singapore. And then:

. . . . . .

"Gray, remember the fights you were having with Jean before you left home?"

"Yes, I sure do."

"Do you remember what they were about?"

"We were trying to shut out the pain of separating by making being together more painful."

"And what did I tell you to do?"

"It was something about being grateful for the moment, wasn't it?"

"Yes. Do that now."

So I did. To this moment I recollect those people with deep affection. They are safe with him in this life or the next. We're still close.

AT 4:30 IN THE MORNING Phil and I stood hot and sweaty in the Santa Cruz Airport outside Bombay. In addition, Phil was somewhat feverish from his infected leg that now needed medical attention. We were in a seething crowd, on line, I think, waiting to get to customs, where the officials would periodically take infuriating breaks for cups of tea. (Though I remain mystified how anyone can drink hot tea in 95° heat.)

We were wondering if our host, Bishop I.P. Andrews, would meet us, but we had no way of knowing, since we'd had no communication from him. Would he be waiting for us beyond the screen? And how would get word to him, even if he were there? And all around us jostled a limitless throng of chatty white-clad locals.

It seemed to me like a good time to pray.

"Lord, this is miserable."

"Gray, honestly—where would you rather be? What would you rather be doing?"

"Sorry, Lord. Actually this *is* sort of an adventure."

At length we reached the agent, explained what we were doing, and got our passports franked. Beyond the barrier we were indeed met by Bishop Andrews, a short, heavy-set, deeply serious Indian, formerly a Disciples of Christ evangelist pressed into service as a Church of North India bishop, a position he hated because, as he solemnly put it, the job required that he faithfully "put out fires in grain fields that others got to harvest."

By midmorning we were on a dusty train, heading south to his diocese, coal cinders flying in through the open windows. Phil slept on two seats we'd sequestered for him; by then his leg was throbbing, a swollen, angry red. That left me and my dark-skinned brother mashed together, forced into conversation.

"Father Temple, tell me if you please, what do you think of the praying in unknown tongues?"

· · · · · ·

And rejoicing in Christ that I had the opportunity to assist this remote colleague, I informed him at length as to my thoughts pertaining to the speaking with unknown tongues. "Bishop, I find it a helpful means of spiritual diagnosis. One who dreads the gift or who fears that it will not be bestowed is often found in need of spiritual counsel and healing."

"Very wise, very helpful," he replied. Then he asked, "Father Temple, tell me, if you please, your thoughts on the baptism in the Holy Spirit."

So again rejoicing in the occasion to render assistance to this dear, isolated brother, I detailed my thoughts as to the baptism in the Holy Spirit.

"Very wise, very helpful," he mused again.

Happily sensing that I was not so useless as I'd feared in Singapore, I prayed, "Lord, thank you for letting me be of service to this servant of yours."

"Gray, as you discern, I brought you to Asia to meet this man. But consider that the traffic of information may be flowing in the wrong direction!"

Ooops. "Uh—Bishop, please tell me *your* thoughts on the speaking in tongues and on the baptism in the Holy Spirit."

"Indeed, as you ask . . ."

Later that night, in his guest room I stayed awake until dawn, fatigue notwithstanding, trying to scrawl down as much as I could remember of what he said in that hours-long talk. The conversation was a spiritual football game, hot shower, and post-game massage all rolled into one experience. I can recall few like it in my life—and I could count them all on one hand.

He spoke of learning to pray with *authority*—let faith take care of itself. It is God's alone to give, not ours to contrive; we need to ask for authority as we pray. I didn't need to ask what it would look like. Bishop Andrews was the very embodiment of prayerful authority.

He spoke of the first exorcism he had ever performed. It was going badly, and he experienced a self-conscious panic, fearing (as I surmised) that he'd be exposed shooting spiritual blanks. He told me of how Jesus had answered his cry for help, saying, *"Why are you giving entity to your enemy?"*

He went on to tell me how he subsequently mocked the devil until he fled: "I took my stand, my feet firmly planted. I said, 'Devil, you are dust and ashes beneath my feet. I will stand here and repeat that like a parrot until you flee.'"

Bishop Andrews spoke of how God's throne is erected upon pillars, the praises of God's people (I think that must be an inference from Psalm 22:3: "Yet you are holy, enthroned on the praises of Israel"). He told me we ought always to praise God in all circumstances, since that guarantees our closeness to God's throne. He told me God had offered him a pillar upholding God's throne all his own to grasp—the pillar of authority. He spoke of how authority has not been withdrawn from the church—it is the lost coin in our household (Luke 15:8–9).

He spoke of prayer: of how his mantra (he loved and admired Hindu philosophy) was "I am yours and you are mine," which he repeated until he could hear God reply, *"I am yours and you are mine."*

He spoke of being ill on two occasions and declaring, "I am the child of God and the little brother of Jesus; what place can illness find in me?" On both occasions he recovered.

He told me prayer is playing at the breast of a father we love and trust until we know we are strong and safe again.

He told me also that southern Asians tend more to the visual than to the auditory in their sense of the presence, alerting me to expect pictures in addition to "words."

He never shed his solemn, formal tone in all the days we were together. But I learned to decode his eyes—their corners crinkled often and, when they did, the whole world felt merry.

Humility was my first lesson of the day, but it was only the preparation, shaving the patient's abdomen in preparation for the scalpel.

· · · · · ·

An Abreaction
· · · · · ·

YOU CANNOT SIMPLY go up to a ticket counter in India and say, "Sell me a ticket to Pakistan," anymore than you can go to your local airport expecting to find a direct flight to Havana. I was scheduled to visit Pakistan, but my Pan Am ticket wouldn't work that leg of the trip. I would need to buy a one-way ticket in India for the trip northward.

That required me leaving Bishop Andrews' diocese on a bus bound for Bombay, where I would spend the next two days pulling church-assisted strings to get to their neighboring country.

I took sad leave of the Andrews family and nearly tearful leave of Phil. Phil was to have come to Pakistan with me, but a local Christian physician had treated his infected shin and recommended urgently that he fly directly home. I knew I would miss him. I'd even miss his arguments.

I was grateful that the bus ride was at night. My torpor anesthetized me against the terror of the ride. It is not entirely clear which side of the road they actually think they're supposed to use in India, though the cars steer from the right. They do not use headlights at night, except occasionally as a warning signal, and there are few protective barriers on the mountain roads. I was glad not to be able see out the window.

The discomfort of the bus ride amplified a mounting discomfort welling up in me since I first left the airport for the streets of Bombay six days before. As the sun had risen that first morning, I realized that the indistinct humps in the road our taxi driver was trying to avoid were not evidence of road construction as I had thought—they were *people*, and not all them were alive.

Bombay at the time was estimated to have over a million homeless people. When I heard that statistic, I mused that if even one city block in the United States were in that shape, Ronald Reagan himself would have declared an emergency.

· · · · · ·

I was overwhelmed at the sight of all the beggars, so many of whom were disfigured. I noticed (critically at first) how Bishop Andrews reacted to them, making a dismissive gesture with his hand accompanied by a sound like "pppffffttt!" Within an hour I was copying him.

Even more appalling than the poverty itself was the apparent insouciance of most of the citizenry to the beggars and to those lying in the streets. The sidewalks were crowded with chattering, British-clad bureaucrats walking to work with their briefcases, stepping over the human forms without pausing their animated conversations. It was as though we were of different species, paying as little attention to each other as squirrels pay to turtles.

Abject poverty was everywhere. Even in the small town from which the bishop administered his diocese, there were huge shantytowns—for the "well-to-do" poor.

I experienced a mounting loathing for the people of India—all of them. I regret that now. I no longer feel it, and today I know it was a projection of my inability to manage my own reaction to the magnitude of what I saw. I do not ask you to understand or, worse, share that feeling of loathing. I simply report it because it was there and there didn't seem to be anything I could do about it.

In Bombay, I had planned to stay at a Christian school for two days while trying to wheedle a ticket to Karachi. At the school I was met by the headmaster, beaming with friendly hospitality—his teeth and saliva bright red with the betel he was chewing. That did it. I nearly gagged. I asked him to call me a cab.

I would stay at a Western hotel until I could get my ticket out. Disappointed, he nevertheless politely summoned a cab. I instructed the driver to take me to the most comfortable Western hotel in Bombay.

In the hotel lobby I had to slink my way past elegantly dressed Westerners, Arabs, Indians, and Asians whose Rolls-Royces, Bentleys, and Mercedes-Benz 600s crowded the driveway. These were men and women who could buy and sell me with their pocket money—as far above me financially as I was above the people sleeping on the street.

I stayed the night in a single room at an outrageous rate. I ate room service hamburgers, in contempt of Hindu dietary sensibilities. I went to the bar and ordered a bourbon. But none of it tasted good. Nothing did, not the food, not the drink. I bathed repeatedly in hot water, the first I'd seen outside a teacup in weeks.

I could not mount anything recognizable as prayer as I isolated myself in that room, high above acres of rattan shanties. I more or less whimpered at God.

I wrote in my journal, "So I myself am a fitting target of the loathing I feel for this city. Wandering around wealthy and aimless in the midst of poverty unimaginable in Western terms. Passing through crowds of miserable people can be done very easily, suffering most deeply not from guilt or compassion or horror—but from loneliness and a vague self-pity. Lord, how can you love me *and* all these rich people *and* all these poor people with the same heart? What must we appear to you? Against what background do you see us?"

Jesus remained silent.

The questions festered during the next week while tasks in Pakistan—and the requisite prayer to address them—took up all my energy.

But they came back.

PAKISTAN WAS THE FIRST MUSLIM COUNTRY I'd ever visited. As in Burma, the extremes of poverty were not as visible as in India, so in that sense it felt closer to home. Balancing that though were the five daily calls to prayer from the mosques' minarets. The traffic was as chaotic as India's. As one driver explained it to me, "My teacher taught me to drive recklessly . . . and live." Some drivers honked their horns so constantly that their car batteries ran down, even with the motors running.

The bishop in Karachi, a native of Norway, had been at the Singapore conference and we had begun our friendship there. I had also met and been befriended by one of his leading Pakistani clergy, Emmanuel. Our embryonic mutual trust began to bear fruit from the beginning. Once again I wasn't sure I'd be met at the airport—it was nearly impossible to send telegrams between India and Pakistan. But there in the seething crowd awaiting the arriving passengers was Emmanuel's beaming face.

The pace of that week was frantic. Emmanuel and I stepped out of the cab from the airport directly into a meeting of the cathedral community already underway. On walking in I learned I was the featured speaker.

By now I had learned a lot about mission stations—and Karachi was no different. Suspicions and resentments choked the spiritual air. The bishop was Norwegian, his staff British, Australian, and Pakistani. I never actually heard the word "wog" spoken but felt it hovering. I quickly ascertained that Australians and English people barely think of each other as members of the same species.

When you're working in a turbulent mission community for only a few days, there is no time to teach lofty subjects like biblical hermeneutics or form criticism. You simply roll up your pants, wade in, and announce, "Jesus says *forgive* each other—it says so right here in Matthew."

. . . . . .

Remarkably people often do forgive each other—and appear to mean it. That's the part God does. Visiting teachers don't have that power. No matter how eloquently they speak, no matter how long they stay, no teacher has the power to change a listener's heart.

At the conclusion of a session with the bishop and his staff, I was startled when the bishop fell to his knees and asked that I pray for his absolution. He wanted forgiveness for gossiping. I wondered briefly what some of the Westerners, so critical of bishops at Singapore, would make of his sincere humility.

At times during my pilgrimage, I felt a breathtaking proximity to Jesus, as though I were under the sink and he were right there handing me the monkey wrench. (Come to think of it, at one point I did repair a toilet for my hapless British hosts, though that task took more profanity than prayer.) Often in conversation with groups of people, when I needed more wisdom than I possess, I withdrew inside briefly, and I'd be told what was going on, what I needed to say.

For example, the bishop asked me to help adjudicate a scandal involving two leaders of a Christian student group who, on the basis of a "revelation" (evidently a vision occurring during a time of lengthy prayer), had lodged an accusation of adultery against a visiting Sikh evangelist. This was especially troubling since the evangelist had been invited by the diocese to come offer a mission. The bishop was naturally annoyed at the students and clearly wished the whole matter would go away. When I prayed for wisdom and discernment, I distinctly heard our Lord say, *"Do not confuse experience with maturity."*

I didn't know what to make of that until I met with the students themselves and with the puzzled diocesan staff. To my surprise, the students, though not so experienced as the well-known evangelist, had a maturity about personal boundaries that the gentleman had not yet attained. In fact his presumptuous dealings with some of the women who had attended his sessions did prove to have been inappropriate.

That saying about maturity versus experience also seemed to immunize the staff against "every wind of doctrine," that is, they had a healthy caution toward all the teachers (like me) who'd blow through the diocese for a few days, lay down some teachings, then leave. The locals might not have all the war stories the visitors reported, they might not be able to report all the miracles the visitors claimed for themselves, but they *could* trust their own maturity.

At Emmanuel's church, things popped each time we had services together. A teaching on reconciliation produced a dramatic result one evening: a woman who had been bitterly divided from her in-laws was tearfully and loudly reconciled with them all. Then the whole bunch of them came forward to receive healing prayer for high blood pressure. That combination made sense.

Everything Bishop Andrews had taught me about prayer served me well. I learned that authority in prayer is not a subjective feeling one has to contrive; it is simply God's gift waiting to be opened.

I also came to appreciate Bishop Andrews's observation that the peoples of the subcontinent receive visual images from God, in contrast to our Western expectation of "words." After I had spent a few weeks in this part of the world, some sort of subconscious leakage seemed to take place—and I found myself sharing this visual experience of spiritual things.

I got used to hearing about images as we prayed together. After a while, when I prayed for people, images began to form for me as well. My companions listened to my description of these images with great delight. Wanting to exploit my new-found gift, one of Emmanuel's lay leaders insisted I pray and get a vision for him—in front of the congregation. I broke a sweat, begged Jesus for a vision, and got one—the man was standing tall in front of God's throne with Jesus' hand resting approvingly on his shoulder.

I wasn't sure this wouldn't complicate my friend Emmanuel's life as his pastor, so I muttered under my breath, "Lord, was that you or did I fake it?"

"Well, Gray, look how happy it made him."

MY TIME IN ASIA had only a few hours to run. The mission part of the pilgrimage was over. My new friends in Karachi offered me a celebratory banquet the last evening I was with them. Then Emmanuel took me to the airport and dropped me at the international departure lounge to board a flight to Frankfort am Main.

My visa expired at midnight, but I wasn't worried—I was on my way back to the West.

My worry-free state dissolved in a hurry at the ticket counter. A BOAC strike in the United Kingdom had backed up flights all around the globe. My own flight would be overbooked in all classes. The next Pan Am flight westward was two days away, after my visa expired.

"Lord, help! Get me out of here," I prayed. And so began an hours-long spiritual struggle.

"Gray, I want you to fight your way onto that flight spiritually."

"How on earth do you fight for an airline seat spiritually?"

"You obey me and resist everything you recognize as a temptation."

The first temptation seemed so plausible. Robin and his wife, my hosts, were close friends with a member of the cathedral, who was a highly placed official in the Ministry of Transportation. A simple phone call would mobilize his efforts. . . .

" . . . And confer an unfair advantage to you over other passengers."

Rats!

The next test came as an obedience:

"Gray, it will be cold in Germany; go to the men's room and dress in your woolen clothing."

"Lord, it's ninety degrees Fahrenheit in here!"

"But not there. Do it."

I did it.

Near me an elderly Pakistani slumped to the floor clutching his chest. People rushed to

· · · · · ·

him, fanning him and loosening his clothes as others called the medics.

"Is that my seat?"

"No. Not that way."

Rats.

A large group of people walked in together and strode up to the ticket window, successfully claiming a thick wad of boarding passes.

"Could one of them have just a wee cardiac flutter?"

"No."

"I hate them!"

"Stop it. None of them has your seat."

A speech suddenly formed in my head. I would approach the ticket agent and say, "Sir, you are going to a great deal of trouble on my behalf, and it could happen that as you do this, some unscrupulous person might ask you for financial remuneration before they will be of assistance. Rather than have you incur expenses on my account, please take this small amount of money from me to use should that occur."

"Gray, cut it out!"

"Sorry."

Hours passed like that. The 3:30 A.M. embarkation time arrived and went. There would be another hour's delay. More and more ticketed passengers crowded into the waiting lounge. At this rate, once everyone boarded, the 747 would look like a circus clown's Volkswagen.

"Gray, do you trust me?"

"I've been trying."

"Go up to the counter now and request a boarding pass."

I did so. The agent said, "I need to call the gate and see if they have a space for you." I could hardly breathe as he dialed.

Through his earpiece I heard a laconic voice say (in English), "Take him."

I grabbed my boarding card (first class), checked my bags, rushed aboard, found the last empty seat and buckled in.

Just then two officials boarded with an irate Pakistani. They walked up to my row . . . and unseated the man across the aisle from me, replacing him with the complainant.

"See?"

ONCE THE KARACHI-FRANKFORT FLIGHT was safely off the ground with me aboard, I slurped down a hasty Bloody Mary and fell into a deep sleep.

It was still dark out when I awoke. I looked through my bag for a book. No luck, I'd read them all. I poked around in the pouch in front of my seat, but I had already read the in-flight magazine cover to cover. I grew frightened. Thoughts of India, postponed for days, loomed on my mental horizon. Now I had nothing to occupy my mind and, without the distractions of Pakistan, I could no longer avoid thinking about India—more to the point, I could no longer avoid thinking about my reaction to India.

I reluctantly began to brood on the questions I'd so sullenly addressed to Jesus from my expensive Bombay hotel room high above the slum, the taste of bourbon stale on my tongue: What can God mean by "human" if the low-caste, parent-mutilated beggars, myself, the ordinary Indian, and the super-wealthy are all of a single species? I'd smirked at the Brits and Aussies in Karachi who didn't claim each other as kin; hadn't I been about the same—and indeed much worse—in India? If the word "human" somehow embraces us all, is a human being a grotesque biological mistake? Am I?

There were more obvious questions I could have asked. Questions like, "Why am I so scared of poor people? Why do I resent rich people? What should I do with all my possessions? Am I responsible for those poor people?" The questions I actually asked were evasions—the intellectually constipated stuff of undergraduate bull sessions, like "Who am I? What is the meaning of life?" The answers I came up with felt impossible, painful, and practical all at once.

What happened next does not go into words easily. It began as a silent awareness of such plumbless depth that I don't really have words for it. Metaphors having to do with the depths of the sea or the limitlessness of space spring to mind, but the very use of language suggests limits that were, for a brief time, meaningless.

. . . . . .

The encounter itself was wordless . . . yet all my questions were answered. I was drawn deeply into a compassionate affection, a love that tenderly enfolded the beggars and their mutilated children, absorbing their torpid despair, a love that caressed the very corpses abandoned in the streets, a love that actually sympathized with the restless neediness of the super-wealthy, that took delight in the self-importance of the chattering bureaucrats and office workers, that did not shrink from at the self-indulgent angst of a bourgeois American cleric who couldn't handle any of it—a love that embraced even him. The ground-tone of that boundless affection was an acceptance and understanding deeper than all our beings, indeed an understanding that moment-to-moment holds us in being.

I gasped in awed, abashed, utter admiration. I may have asked, "How can this be?" because in apparent answer to my question, I was offered my last vision from Asia.

I saw the vast crucified torso of our Lord, suspended high above the subcontinent, larger than the earth below it, pierced by countless small darts of misery shooting up from the earth. Uncountable shafts of pain penetrated the torso, infinite repetitions of the spear-thrust at Calvary. The loneliness and pain of people abandoned and dying penetrated Jesus. The indolent boredom and social anxieties of the rich penetrated Jesus. I saw Bishop Andrews' anguish over his fractious Indian diocese penetrating Jesus. And the confusion and self-loathing of a suburban priest from Georgia, miserable in an expensive hotel room his parish would have to pay for penetrated Jesus too. And Jesus received all of it, welcomed it.

"Look more carefully."

Back down the arrow-straight trajectories of pain rising from the subcontinental earth there poured life, flowing from Jesus' torso into all the suffering below. Our pains shooting upwards and Jesus' Life answering downwards formed something like cables, preventing the subcontinent from sinking under its own weight of misery.

I stared and stared. The vision did not fade. I was seeing the truth.

"Does anybody down there know about this?" I whispered.

"Not very many, no."

"Does it matter that not very many people know this?"

"No, not very much."

I began to weep, hard convulsive sobs. I tried to smother my noise with a handkerchief, but I think I still alarmed the Japanese gentleman in the next seat.

"Your experience in India has wounded you. It has torn something in you. Do you want me to heal your wound?"

"I think not," I replied through tears. "I think it would be better to leave this wound open and hurting for a while. They still hurt. And you still hurt."

"Thank you. That is what I had hoped you might decide."

. . . . . .

The Fruit
· · · · · ·

A REAL PILGRIMAGE will change you. Certainly I returned from Asia changed. Some of the changes partially "took."

I returned with a resolution never again to use the things of God in an adversarial way. Trying to be attentive to our Lord's presence is a full-time job, leaving little time or energy to rail at others who differ.

I returned with the sense that the great danger to the human creation is tribalism—in whatever form it takes. Racism is certainly our homegrown American expression of it. But it extends to all our attempts to exclude others from our ranks—attempts to privilege male over female; white over color; wealth over modest possession or poverty; marriage over non-marriage or divorce; and (it eventually struck me) heterosexual over homosexual.

The important thing, it seemed to me, was not to level differences between people. For all of its difficulty, that project is finally an expression of spiritual laziness. The real task is to ignore differences, no longer to allow them to count.

Those postures are strenuous to maintain and are not always as warmly welcomed as we'd hope. It's tricky to remember that the task is not to persuade others to those resolutions—it's to live them ourselves in all circumstances.

I discovered in my own spiritual community how hard it is to keep a sense of who God wants us to be without using critical comparisons with others as a prop for our self-understanding.

Our resistance to the presence of God pains me, but it no longer scandalizes me. I know that resistance real well. I have my own list of people I wish God didn't love. When I'm nursing grudges, my heart wants no contact with God's heart. I knew that before Asia—but personal realizations in Asia made it all more urgent and poignant.

· · · · · ·

It would be fun to claim that everyone who knows me notices those resolutions and is impressed with my consistency in living them. If you believe that, I want to discuss some Florida real estate with you.

■ ■ ■

A not very dramatic example of what I mean occurred a couple of years after the Asian pilgrimage.

I had slipped back into the habit of self-location by criticizing people and parties I disagreed with. In that state I was particularly vulnerable to two books I mistakenly read close together: Paul Johnson's *A History of Christianity* and Ute Ranke-Heinemann's *Eunuchs For The Kingdom Of Heaven*. Johnson's book exposes much of the ulterior motivation (did James set Paul up for arrest in the Temple?) and short-sightedness (various groups' attempts to eradicate each other in God's name) that pollute Christian history. Ranke-Heinemann's book is a scorching indictment of the ways the churches have marginalized and persecuted women throughout history.

Those books will embarrass anyone out of their ecclesiastical chauvinism. Together they sent me into a faith crisis in which I lost sight of the point of everything connected with the church as an organization—and with the crisis I lost all sense of access to God.

One day I was driving my car around in that miserable state of mind—and found Jesus was in the front seat of the car with me. His presence absorbed and interpreted my previous despair, offering me a vastly more complex—indeed, a *braver*—grasp of his purposes among us than I'd previously imagined.

I gasped, "Lord, that is absolutely glorious! But help me with something. I am fairly bright, but what you're showing me is beyond my mental capacities to take in fully. What do people do whose heads don't even work as well as mine?"

His utterly disarming reply:

"Gray, I am equally accessible at every level of complexity. "

121

A WHILE LATER JESUS was to show me his accessibility at both a simple and a mind-stretching level simultaneously.

I arrived home late one night from some meeting or other. I was still feeling the warmth of that fresh breakthrough and was happy with the world.

I love where I live. It's still sort of in the country, despite the leapfrog effect of urban sprawl. My house sits in woods facing a broad meadow. It was a clear night, and I could see stars.

I paused to gaze up into the night heavens before going inside. I reflected on some reading I'd been doing on cosmology, that we are the stuff of stars, of the birth, collapse, and rebirth of stellar systems, each cycle producing more and more complex elements until carbon-based life became possible in our neighborhood. I realized that in gazing at the stars I was looking up at the vast cloud of detritus from the creative process that had produced us.

It struck me that the old notion that "Cleanliness is next to godliness" is anal-retentive claptrap. God is too lavish to be tidy. Jane was right to paint the kid's ice-cream cone dripping on Jesus—it was as much a delight to Jesus as it was to the child. Creation is extravagantly messy and wonderfully, prodigiously wasteful. God will scrimp no material in producing us.

Behind and above me I heard a voice. Once again I knew better than to look back. The voice was gaily making fun of the sort of parental scolding that produced my conscience:

"Clean up your room!"—Sounding for all the world as though God's own Mama were fussing.

I could not resist the happy laughter that took me over, laughter shared with the source and final destination of all real laughter in this universe––and I gave in to it.

I love it when that happens.

. . . . . .

122